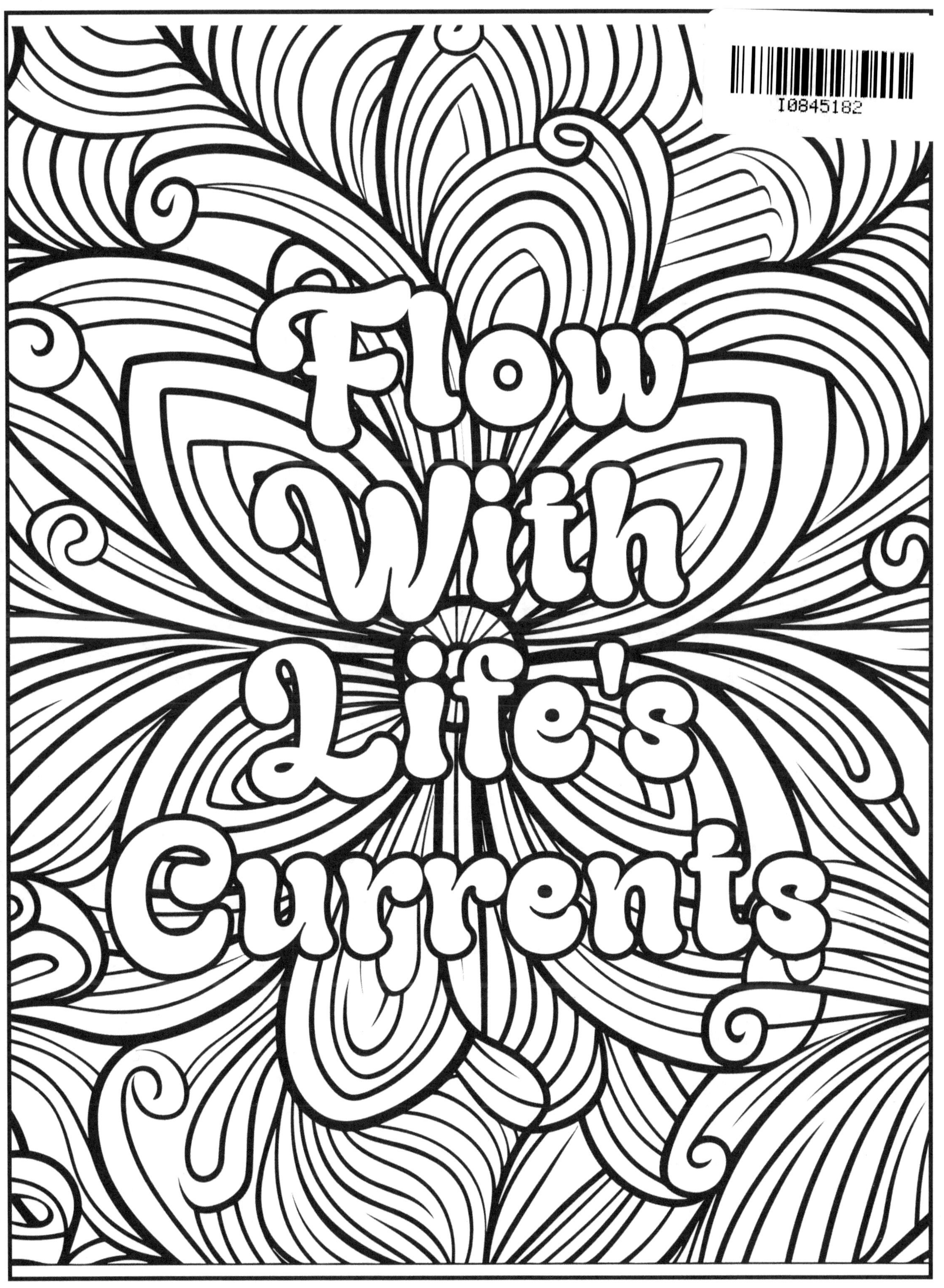

Flow
With
Life's
Currents

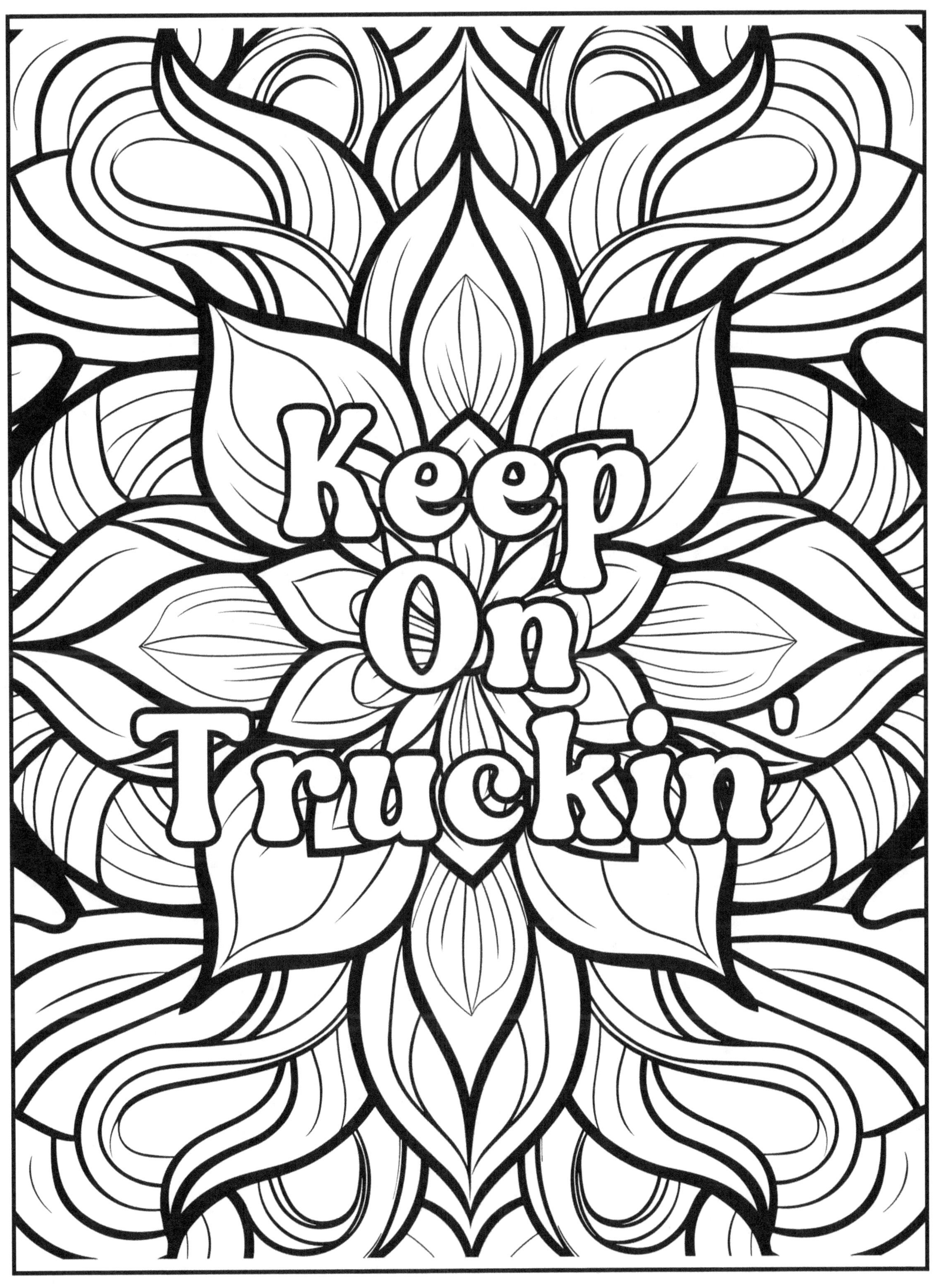
Keep
On
Truckin'

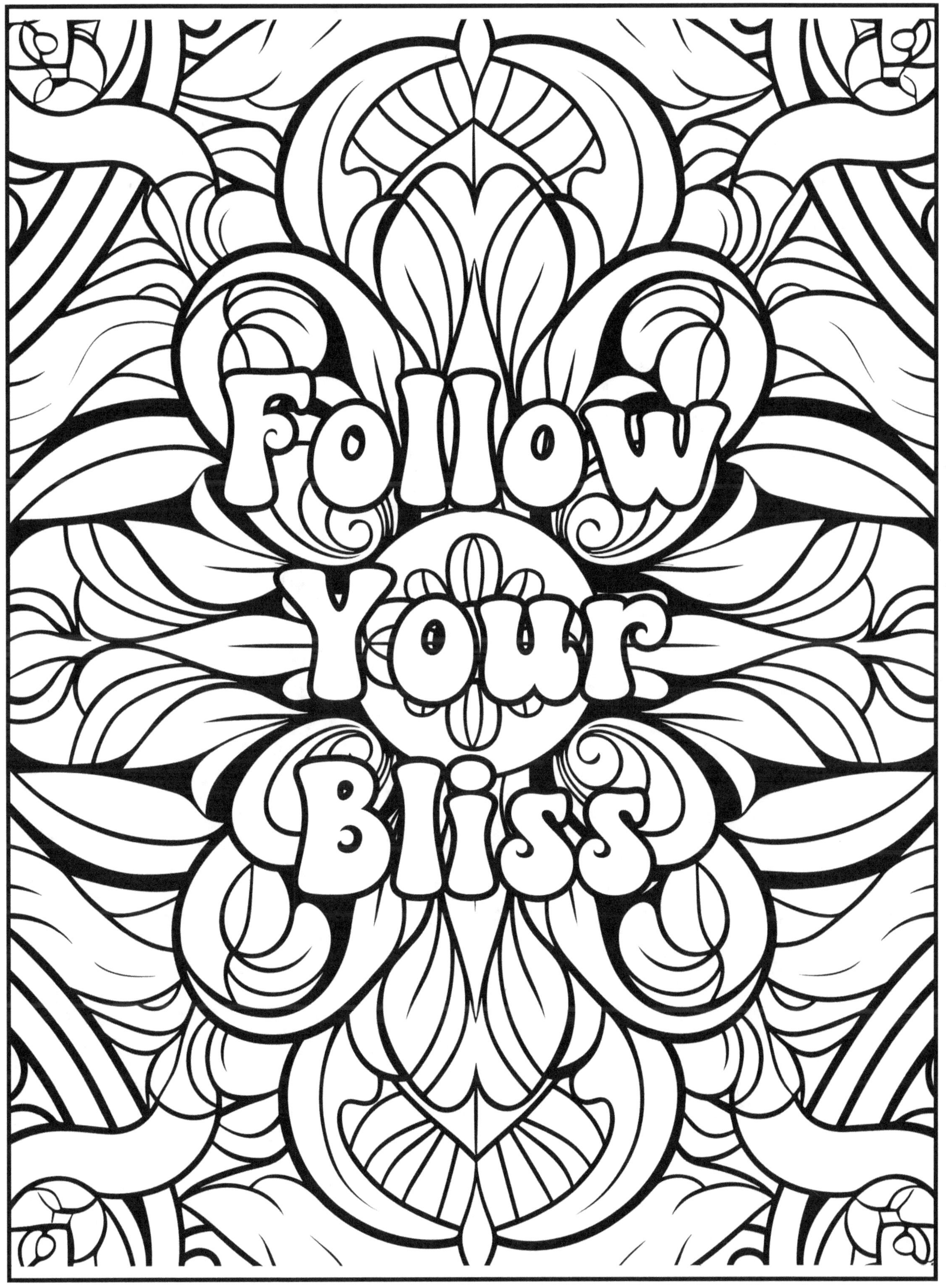

Follow Your Bliss

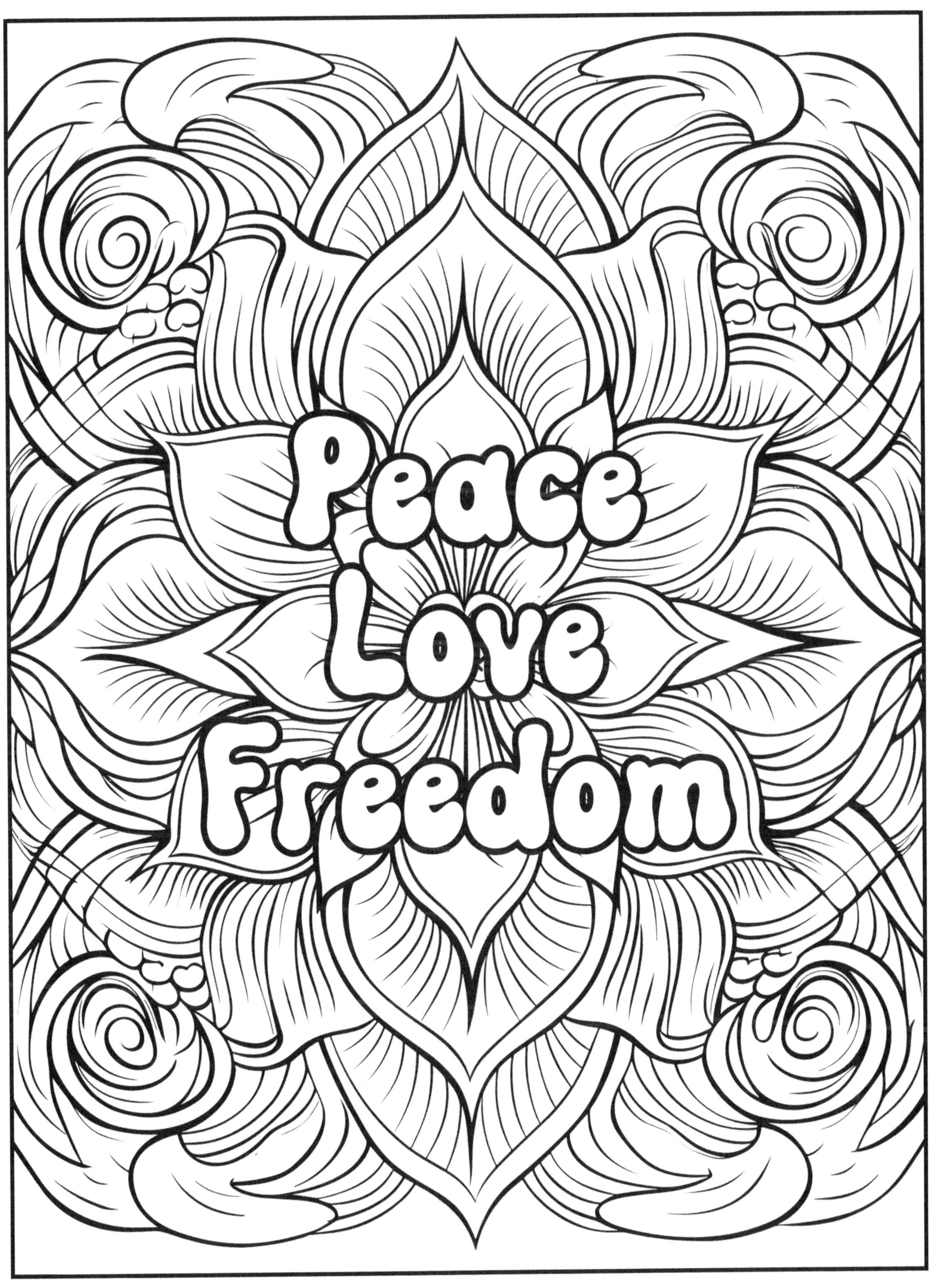

Peace
Love
Freedom

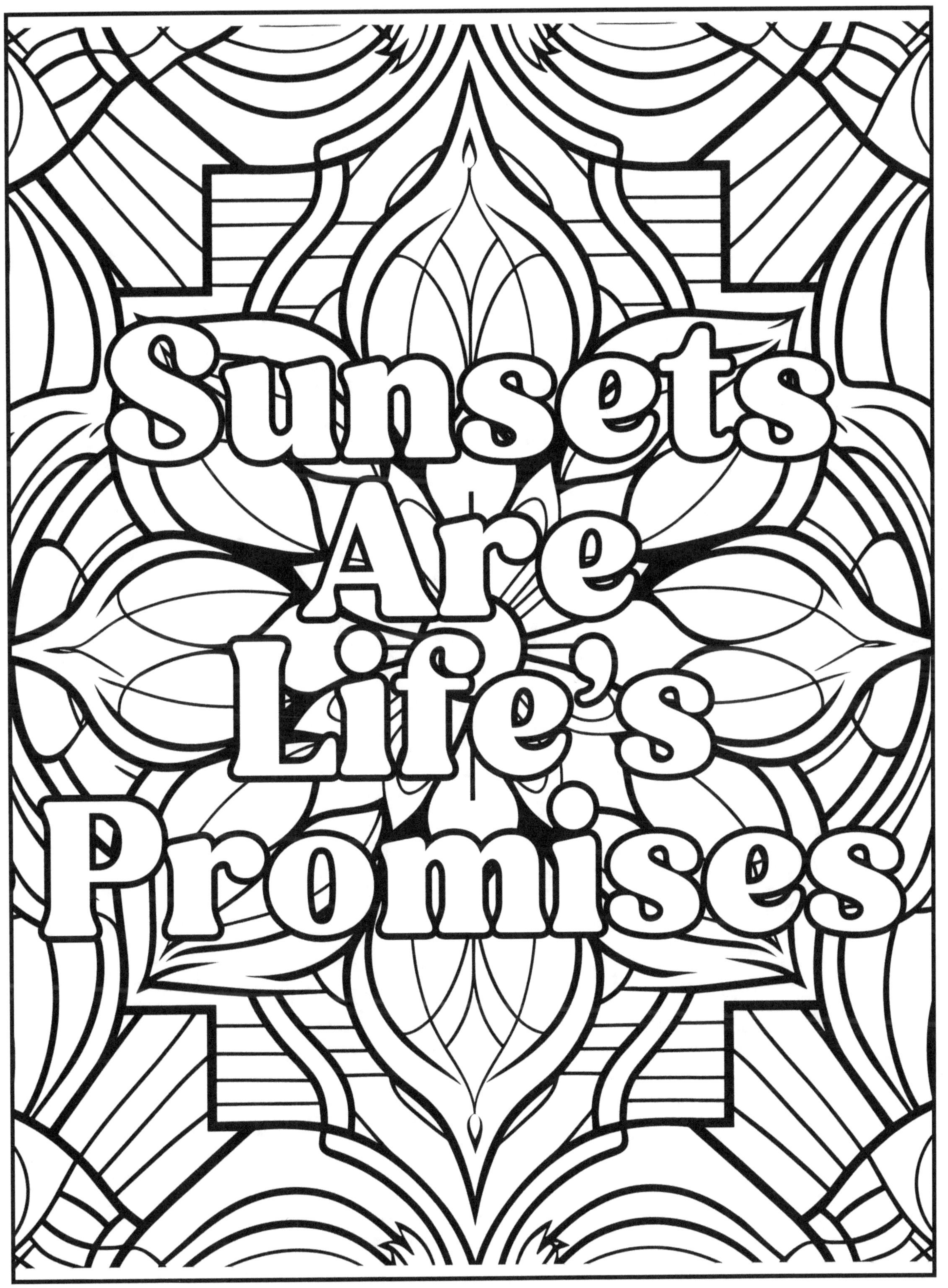

Sunsets
Are
Life's
Promises

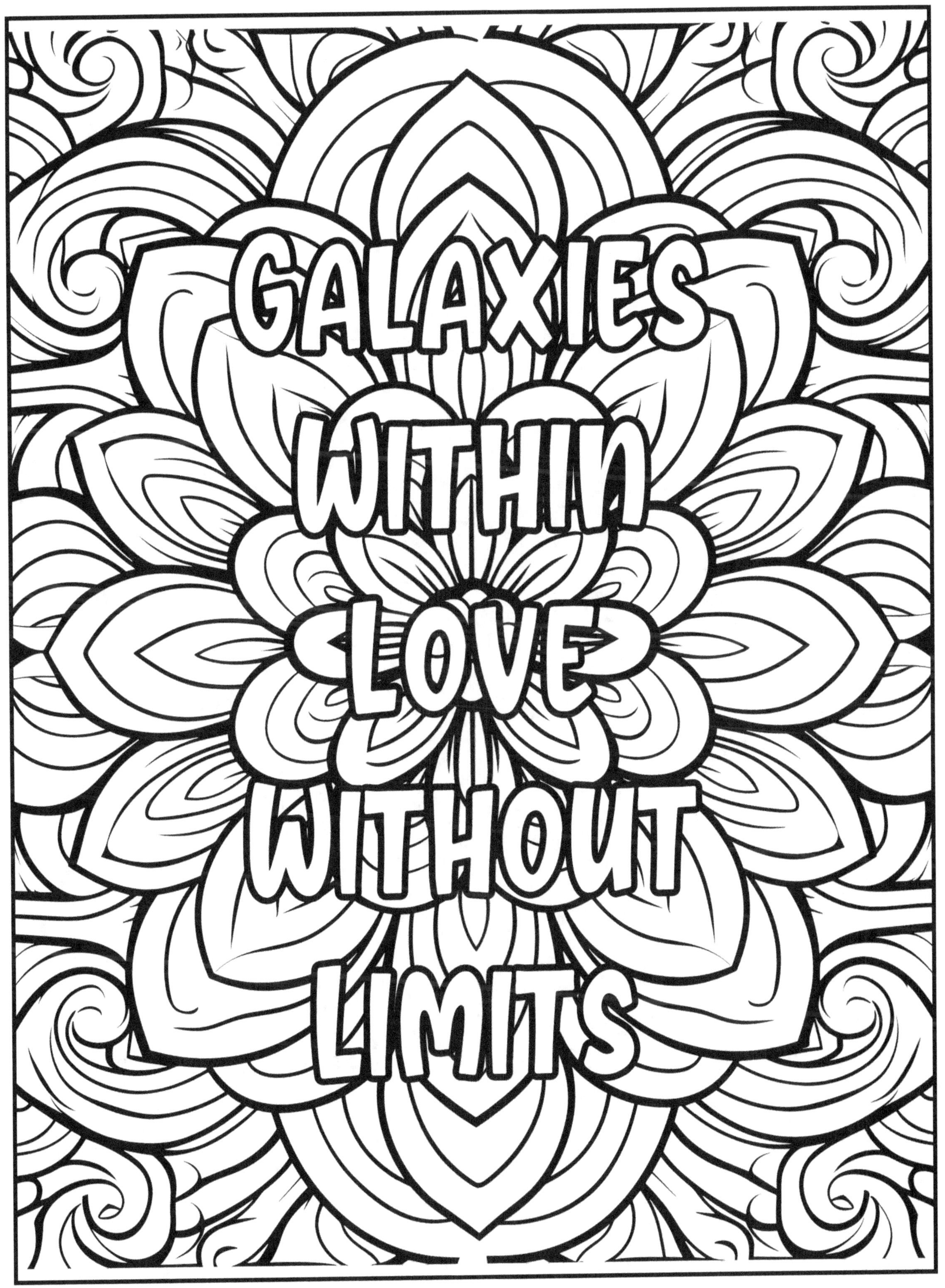

GALAXIES
WITHIN
LOVE
WITHOUT
LIMITS

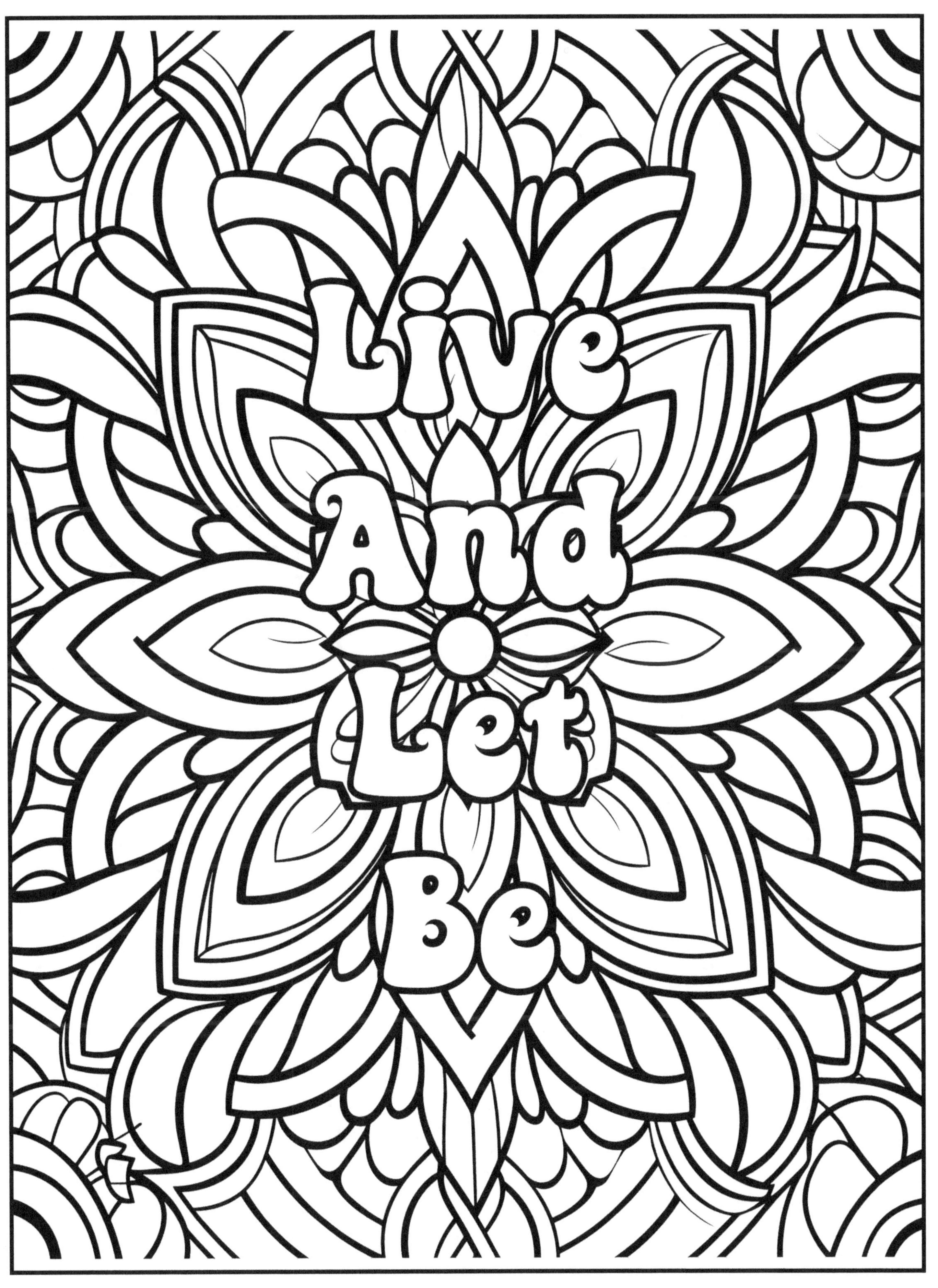

Live
And
Let
Be

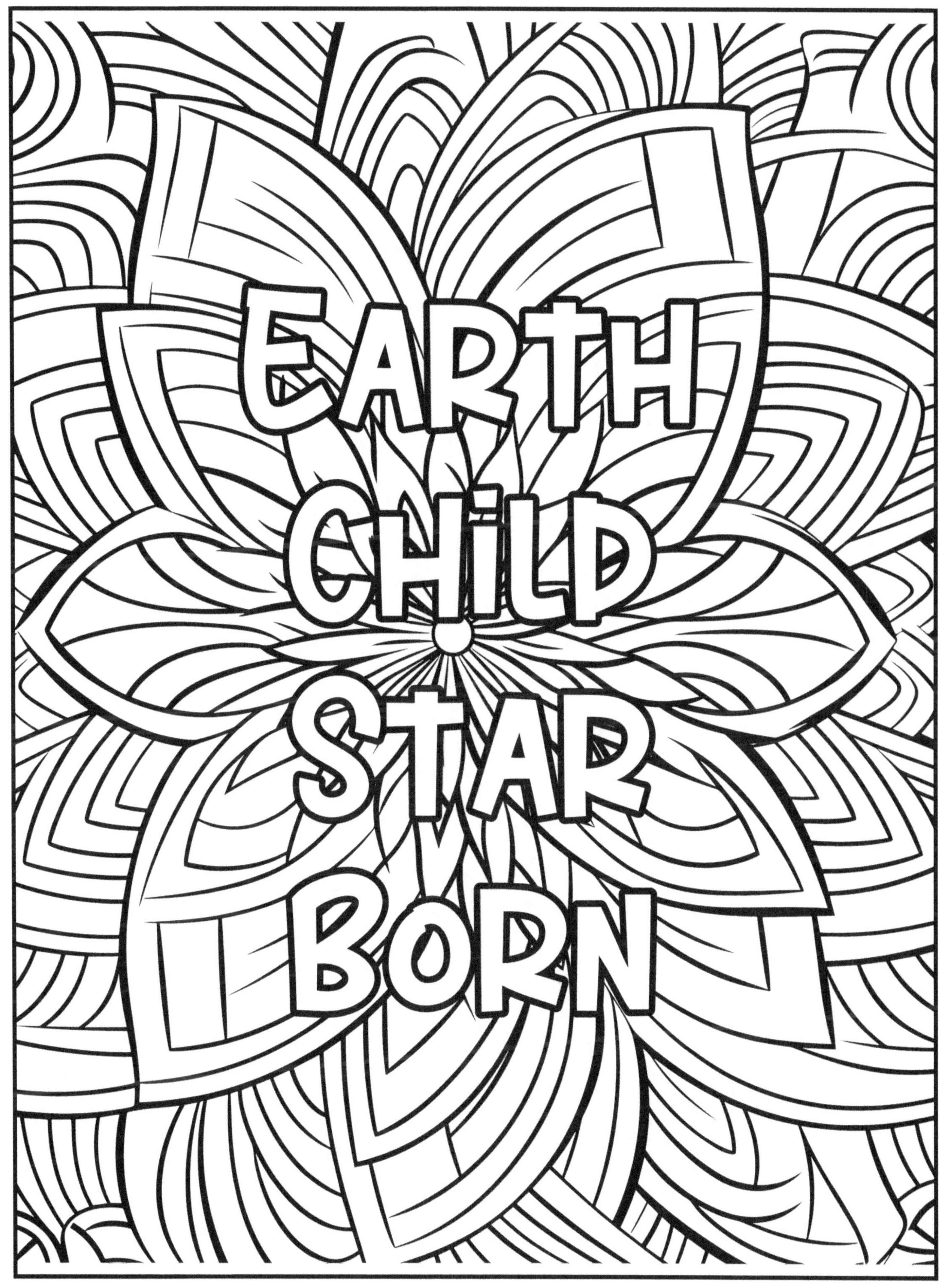
Earth
Child
Star
Born

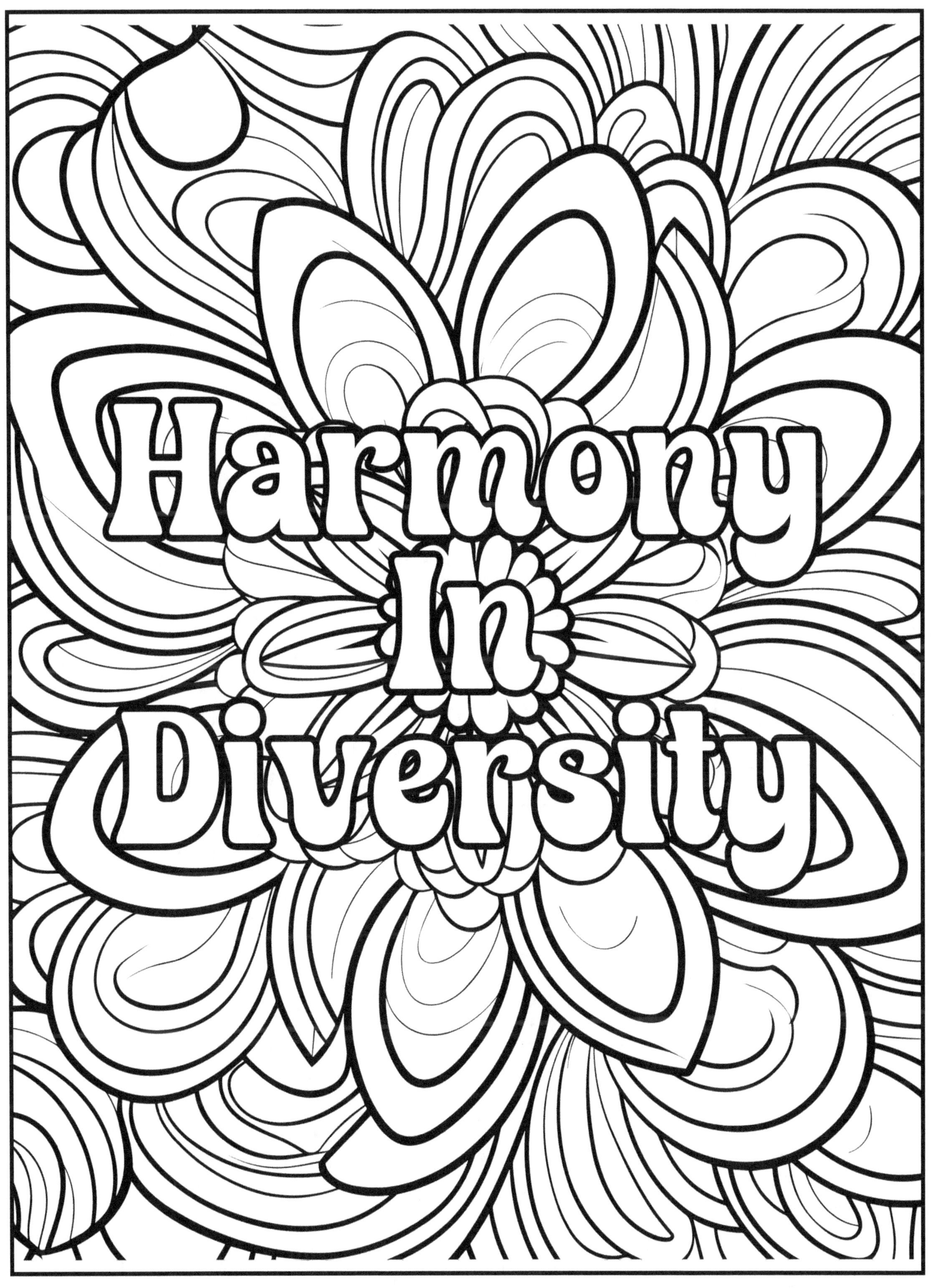
Harmony In Diversity

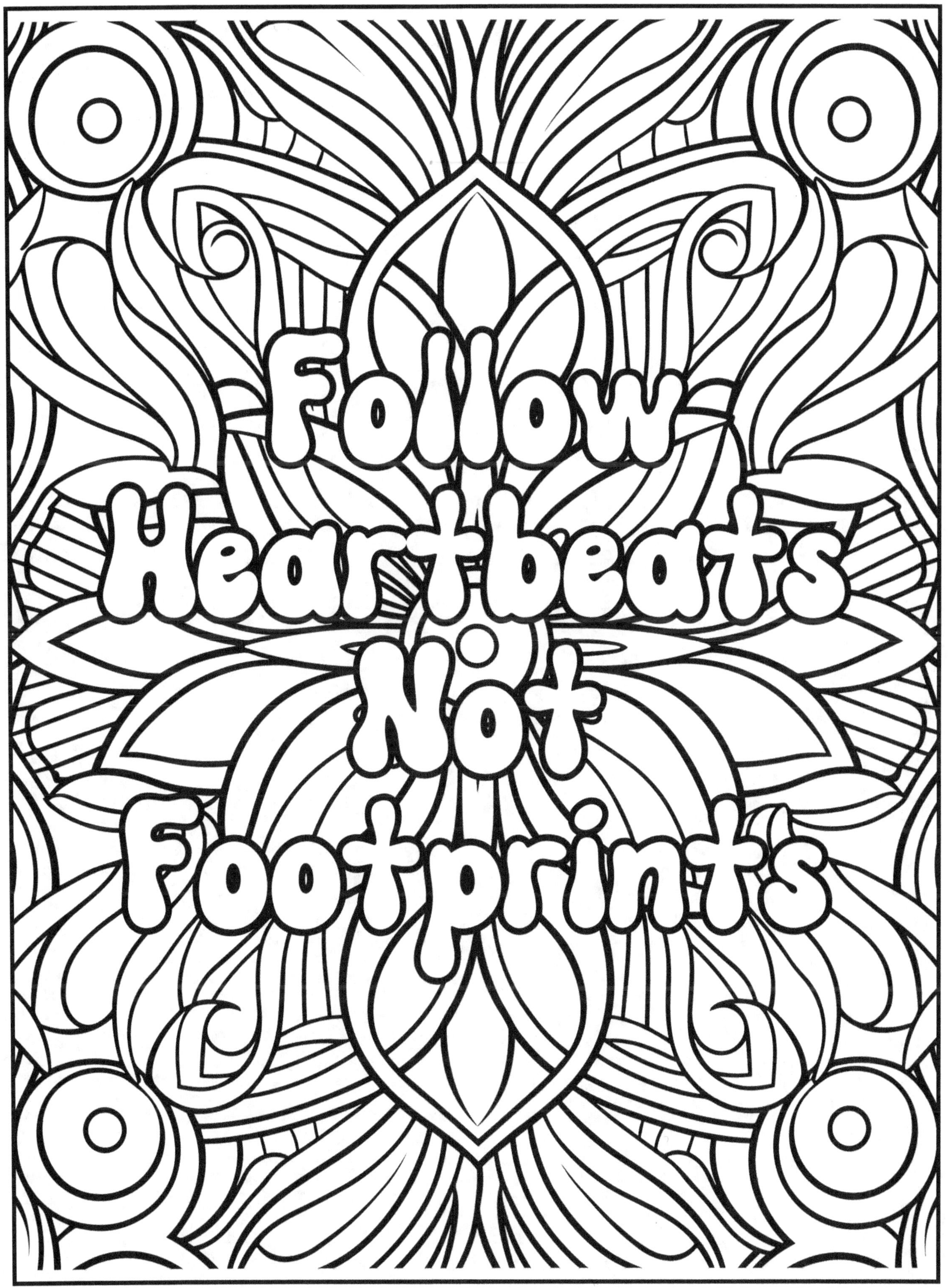

Follow
Heartbeats
Not
Footprints

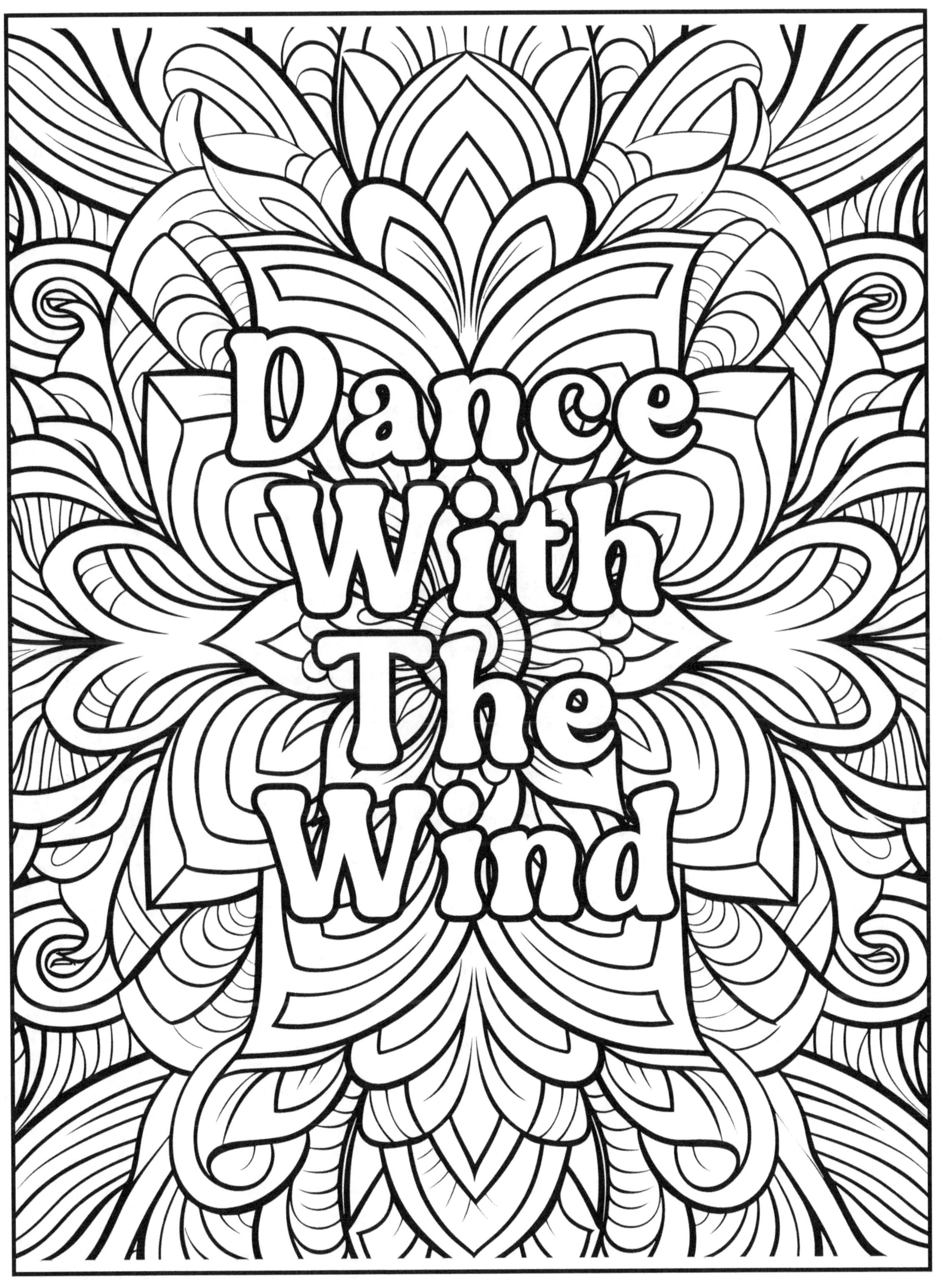

Dance
With
The
Wind

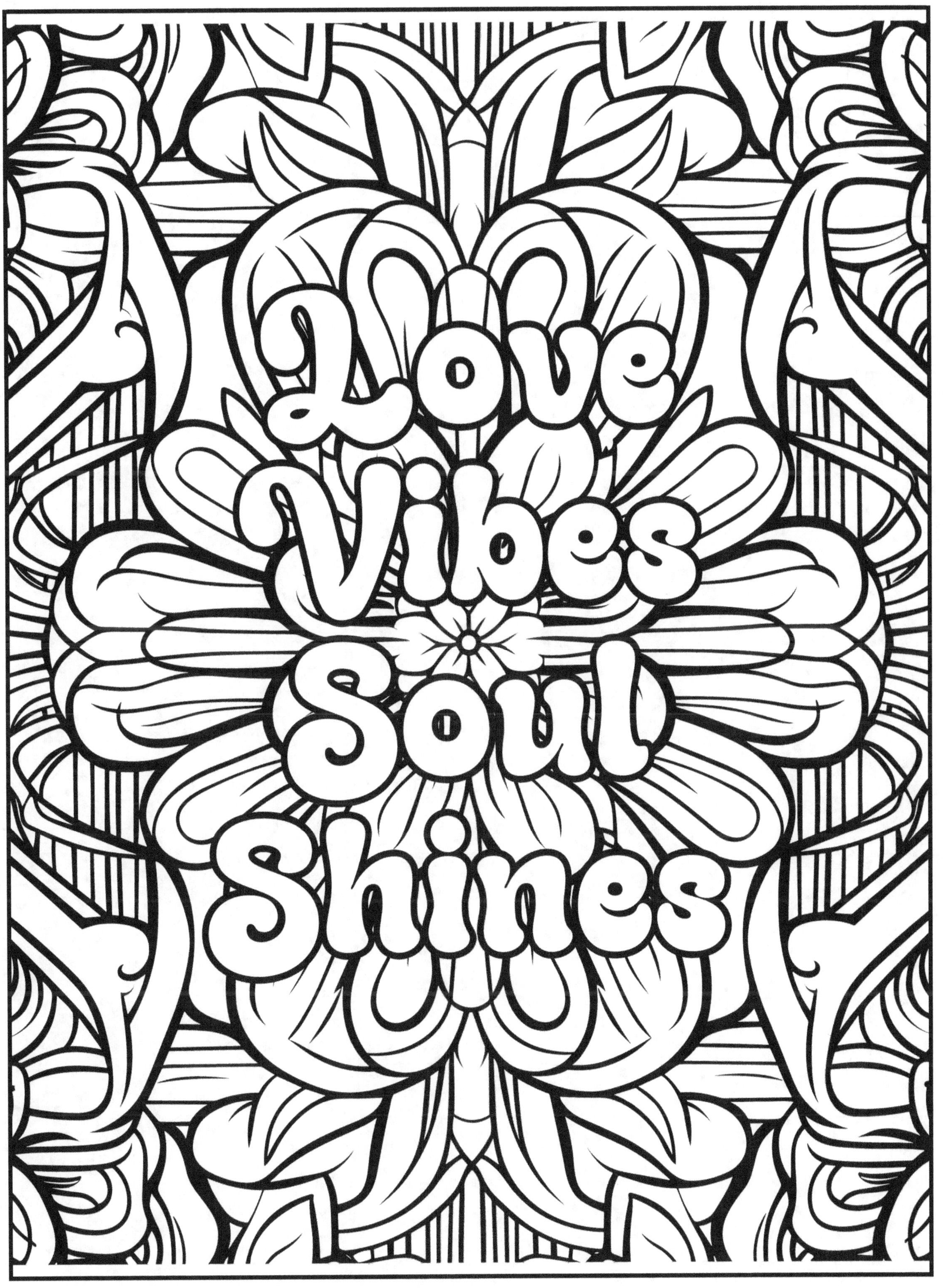

Love
Vibes
Soul
Shines

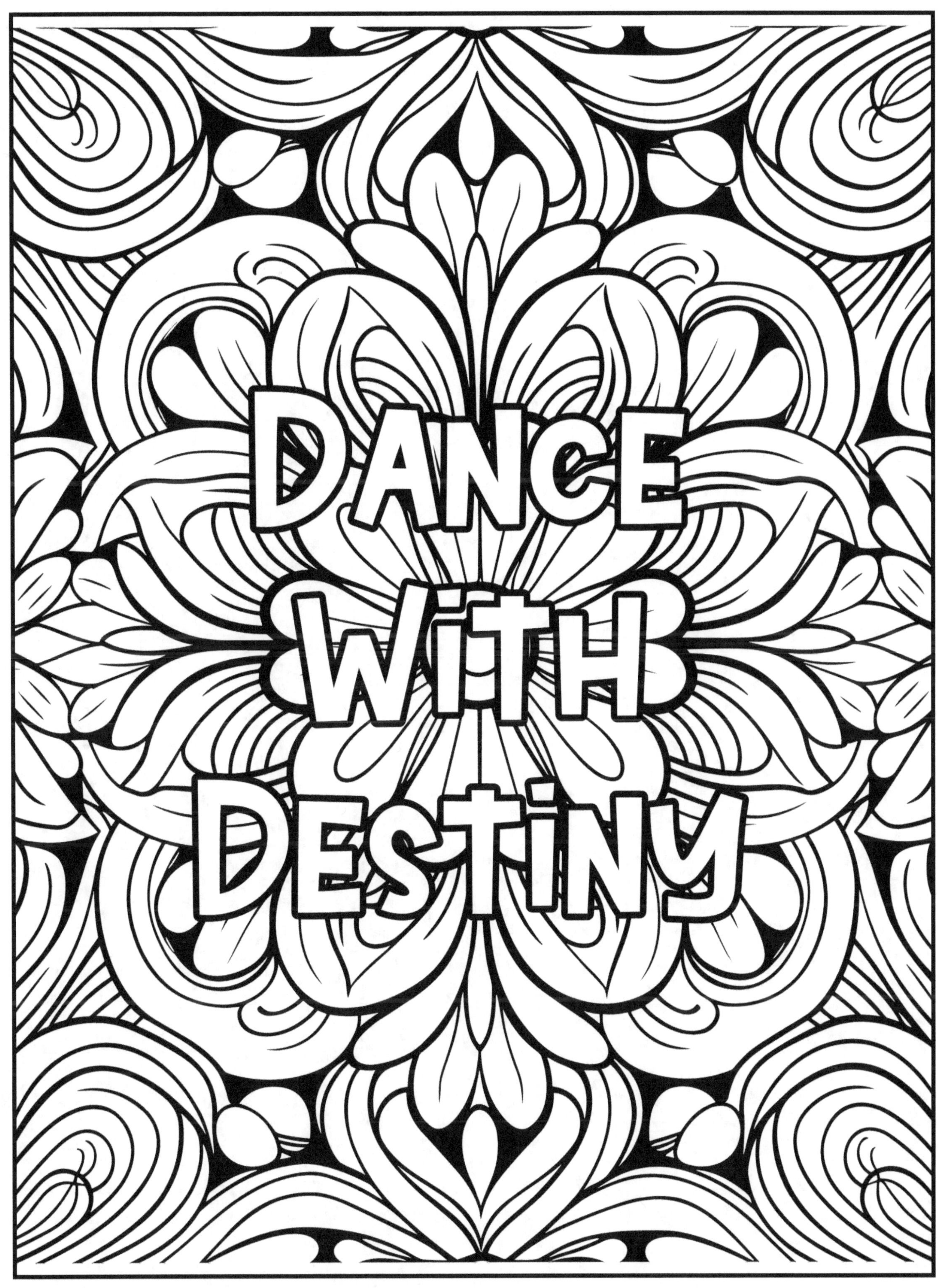

DANCE
WITH
DESTINY

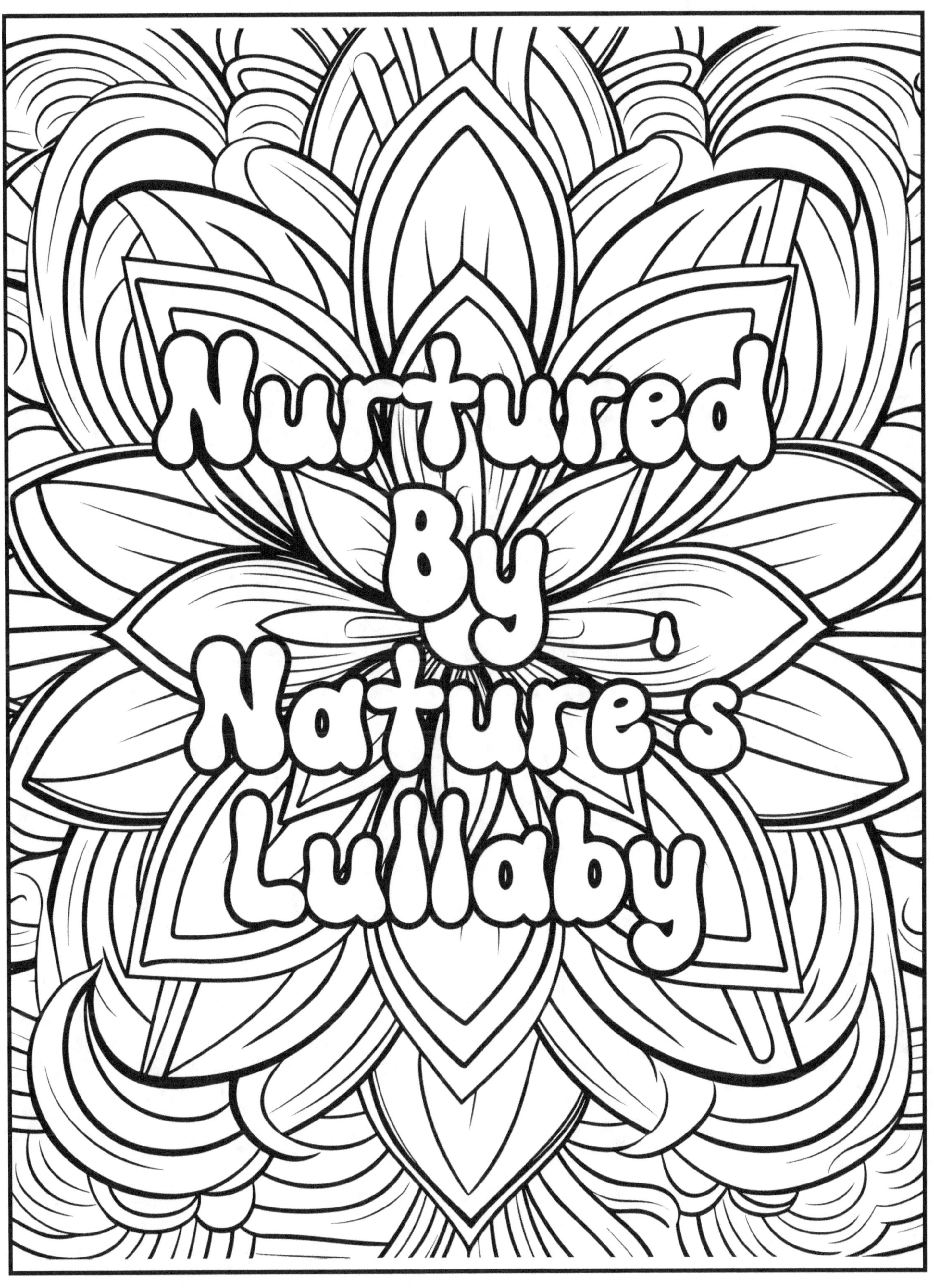

Nurtured
By
Nature's
Lullaby

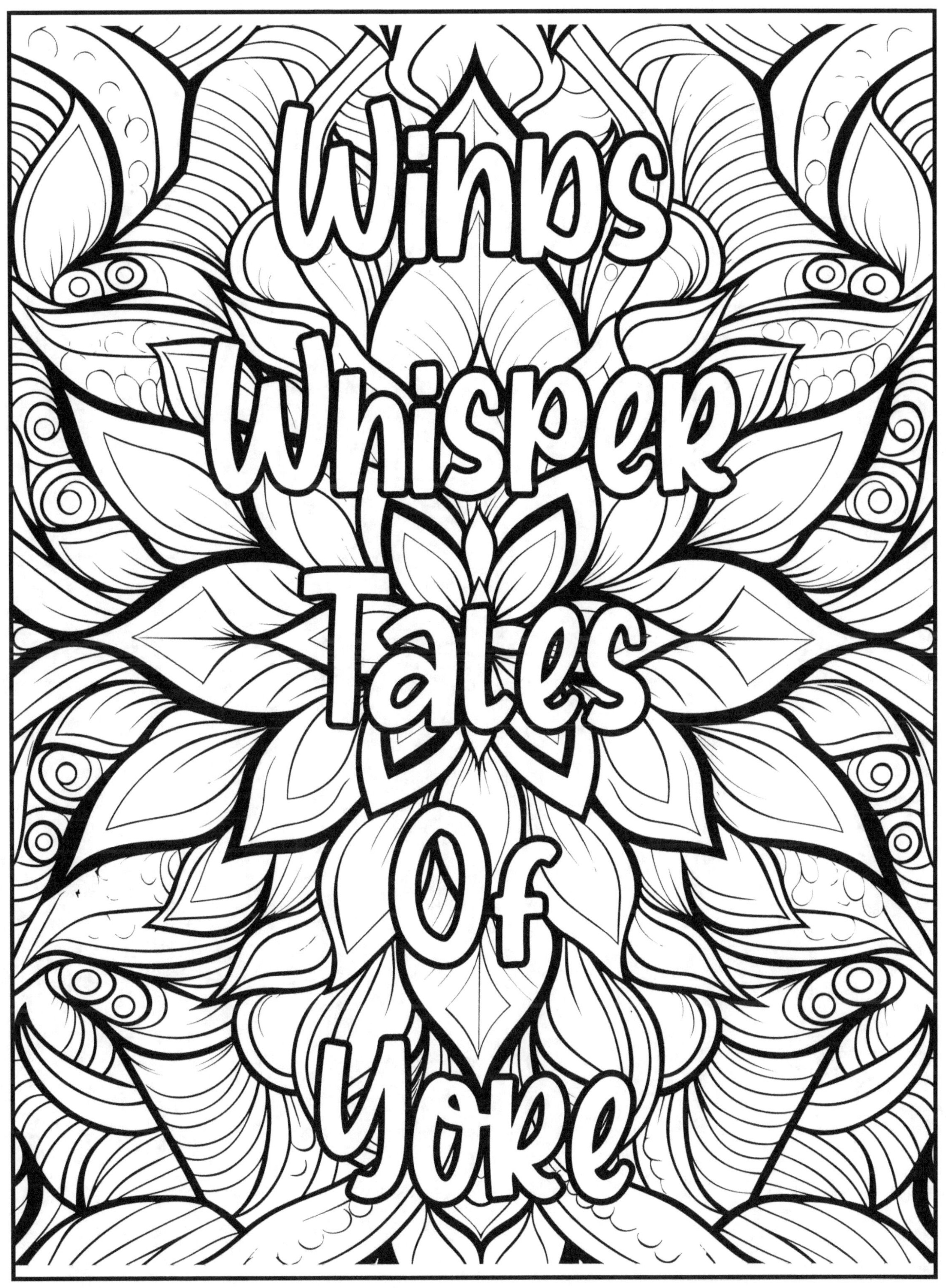

Winds
Whisper
Tales
Of
Yore

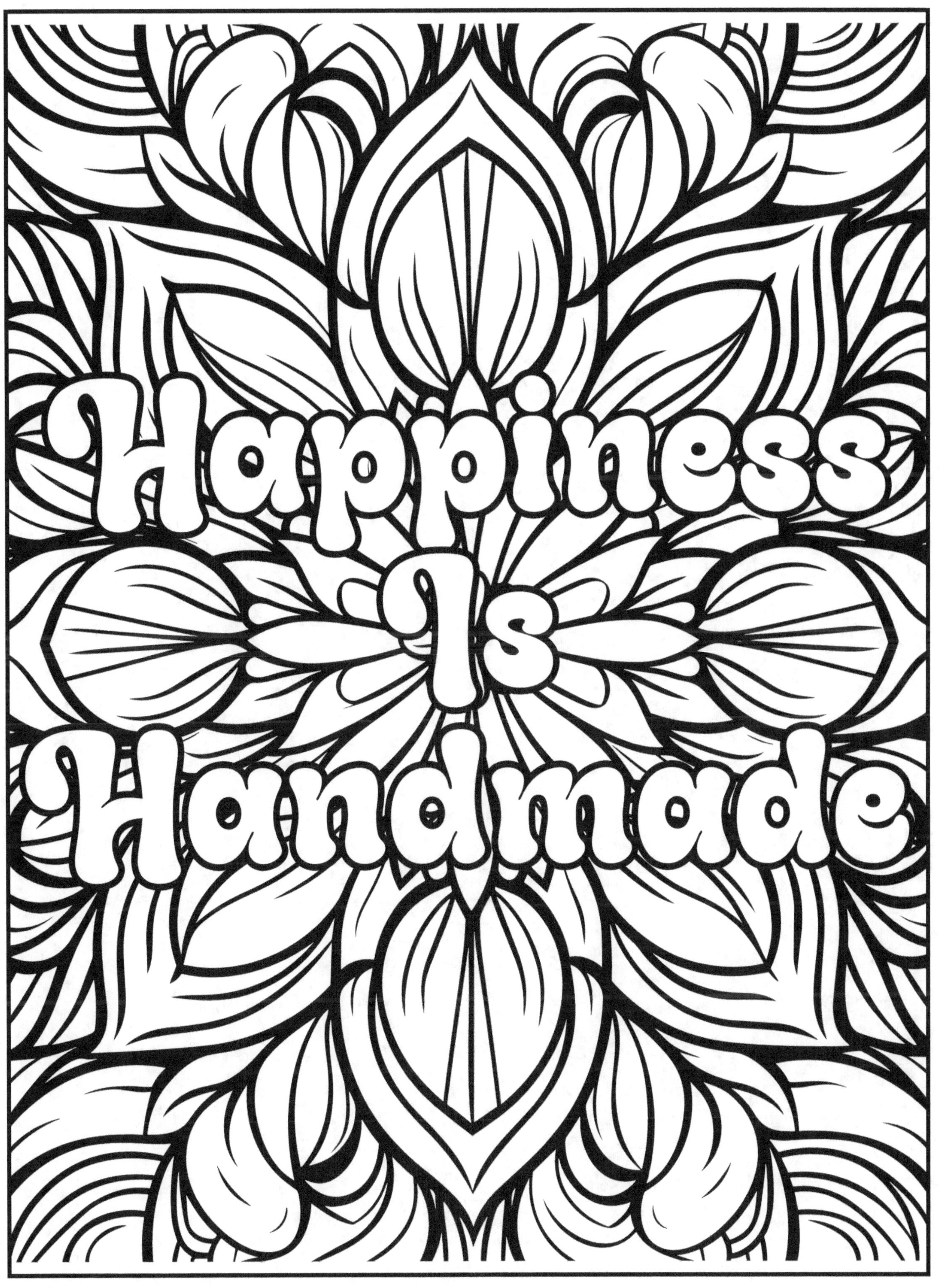

Happiness
Is
Handmade

Seek
Adventures
That
Open
LY our
Heart

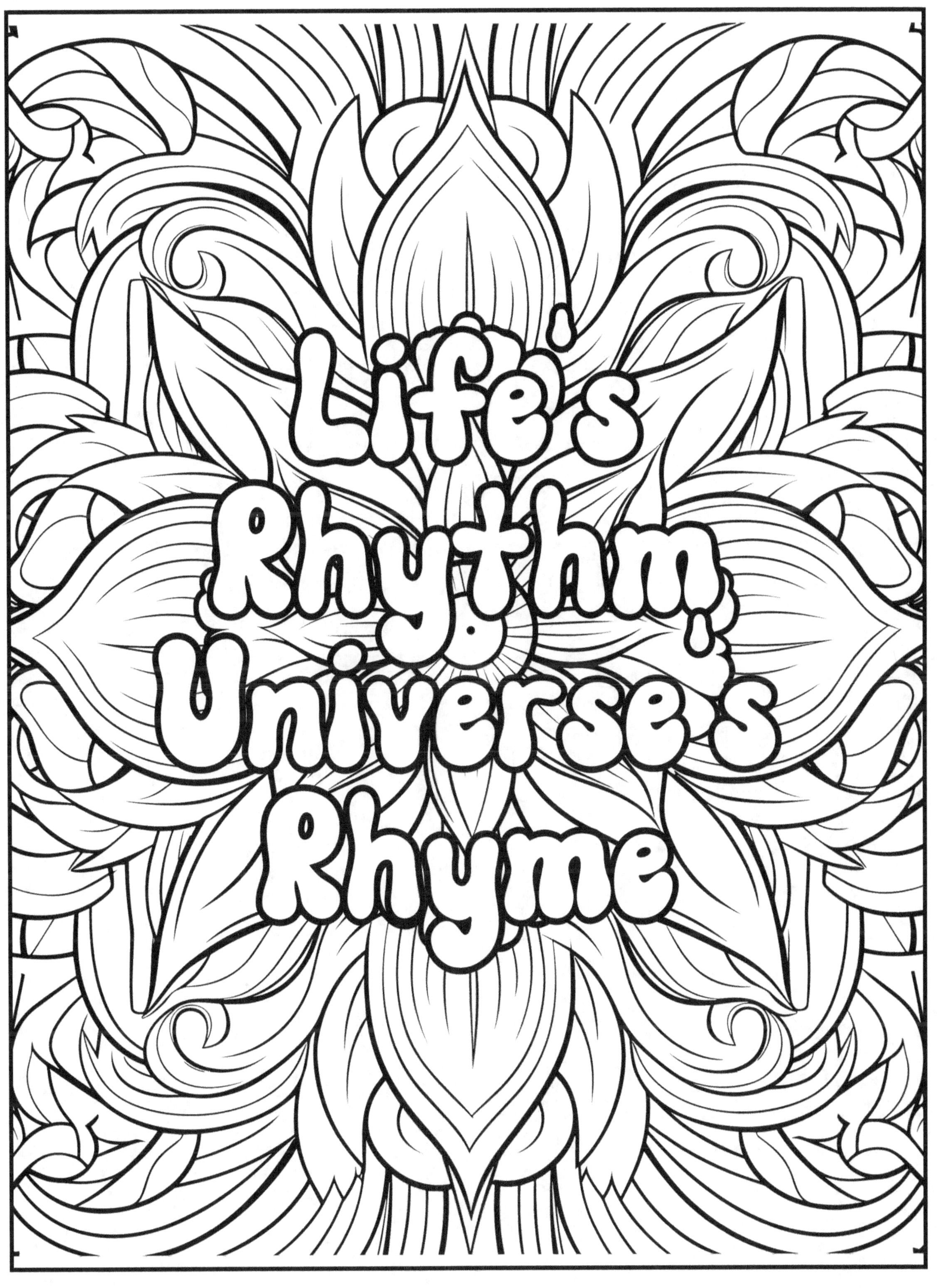

Life's
Rhythm,
Universe's
Rhyme

Feel
The
Universe's
Rhythm

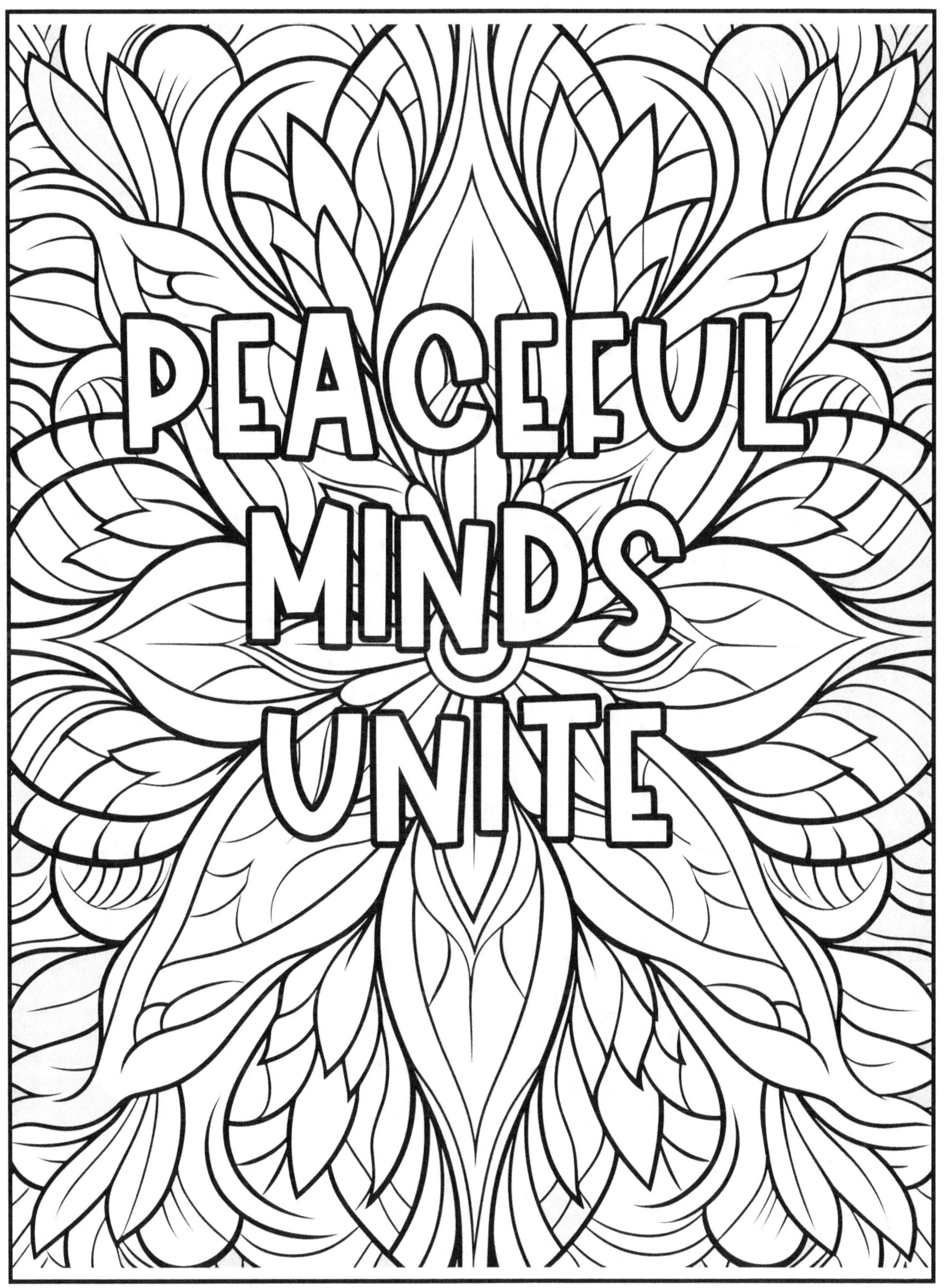

PEACEFUL
MINDS
UNITE

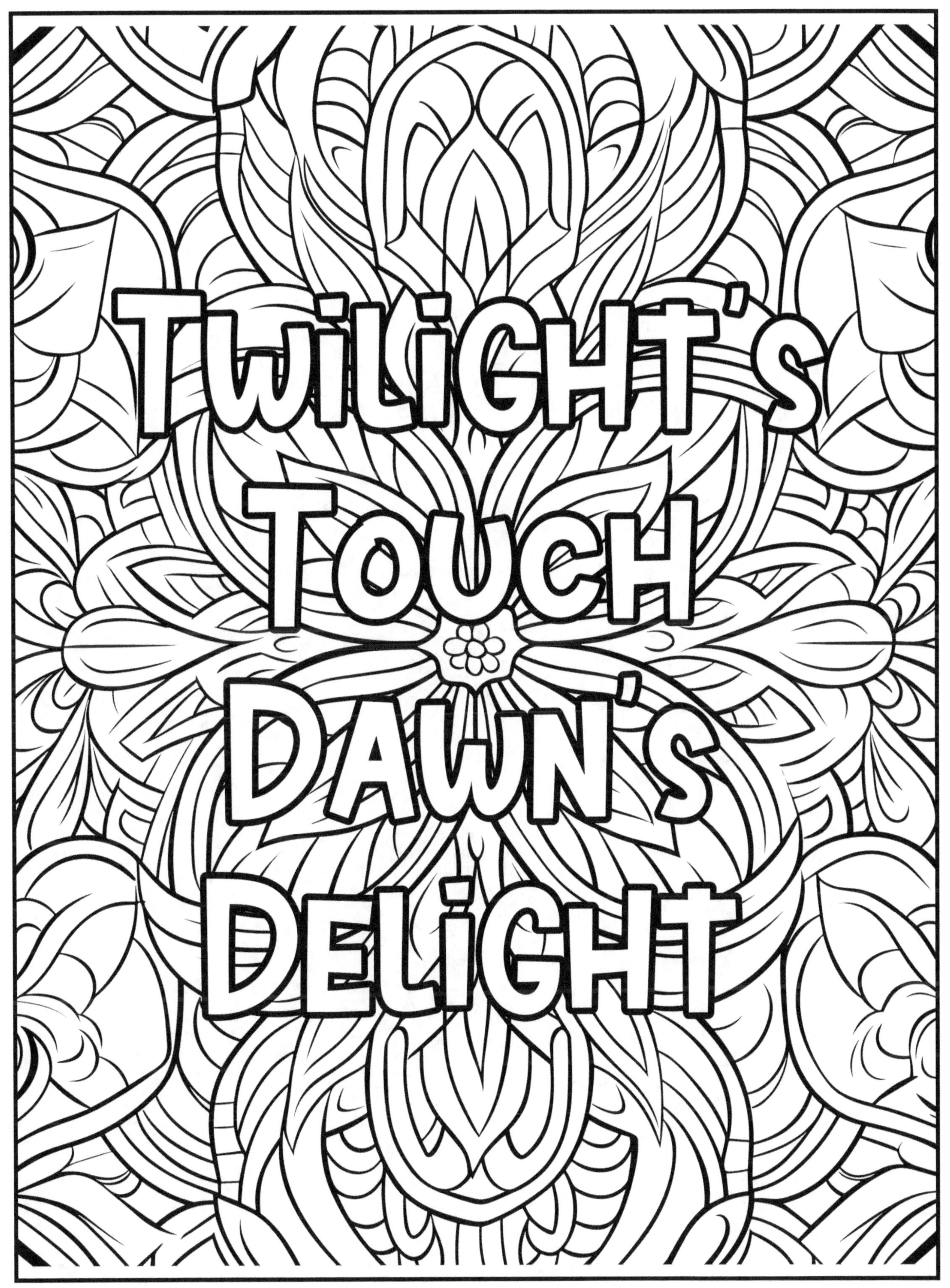

Twilight's
Touch
Dawn's
Delight

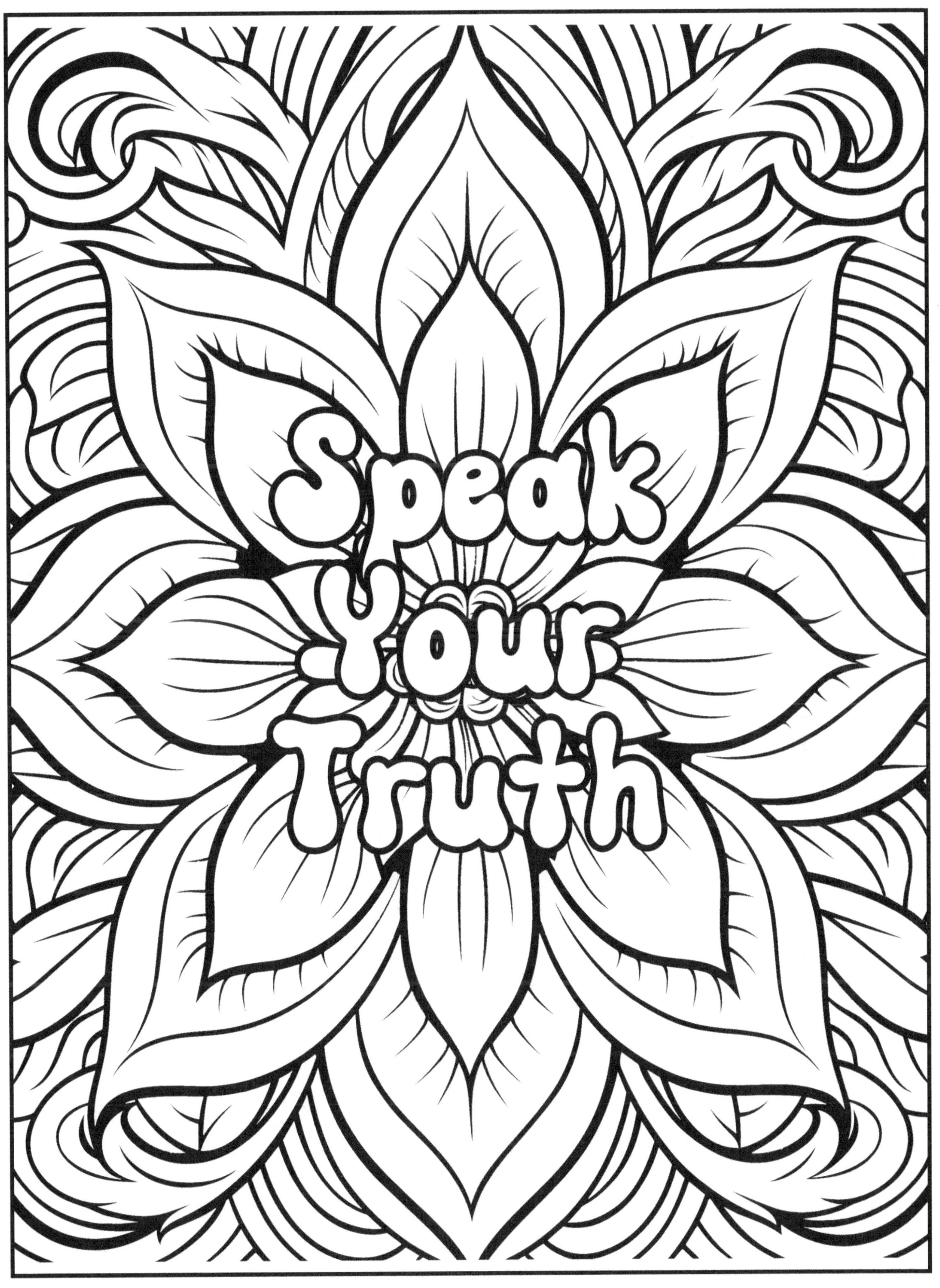
Speak
Your
Truth

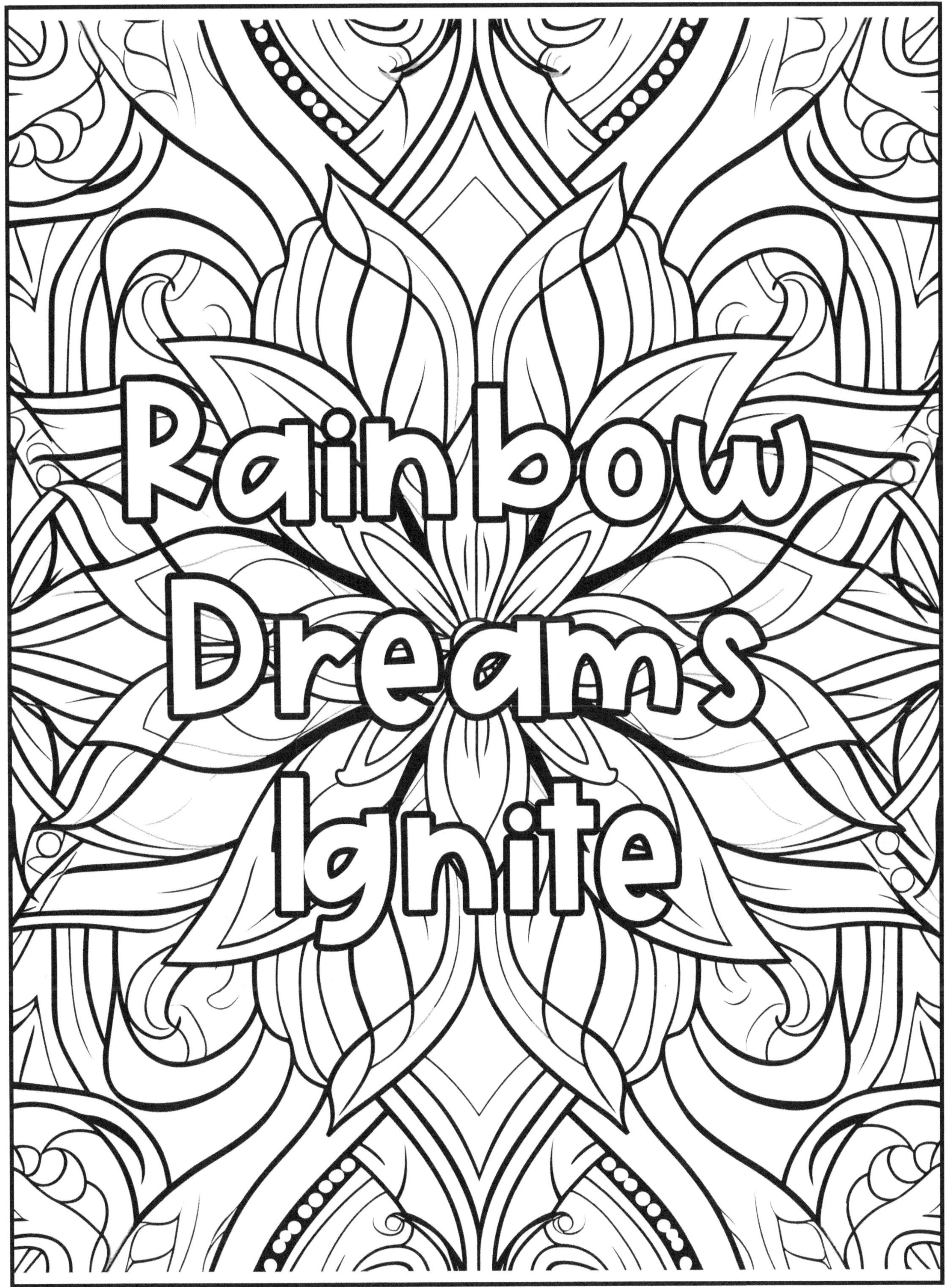

Rainbow
Dreams
Ignite

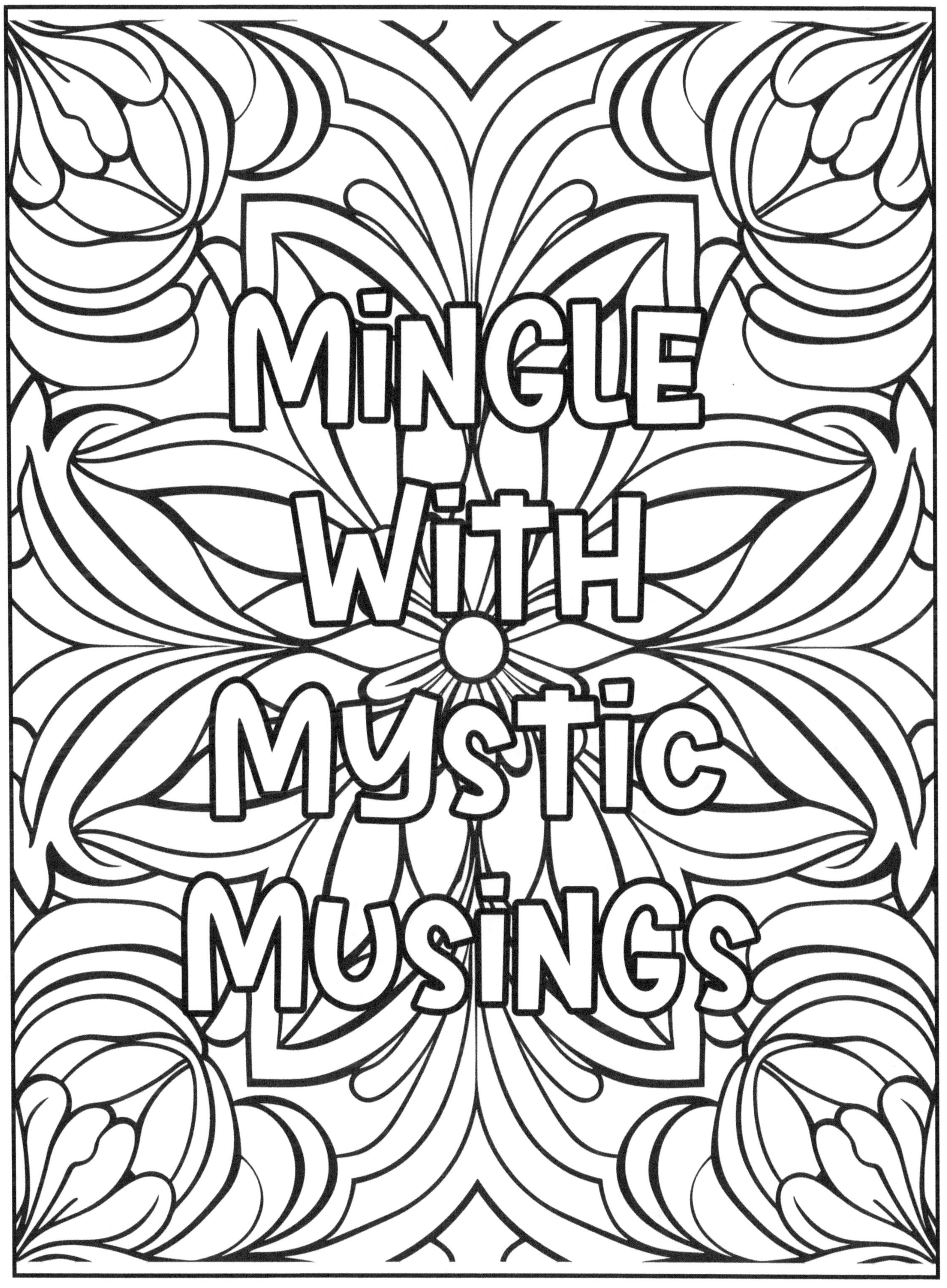

Mingle
With
Mystic
Musings

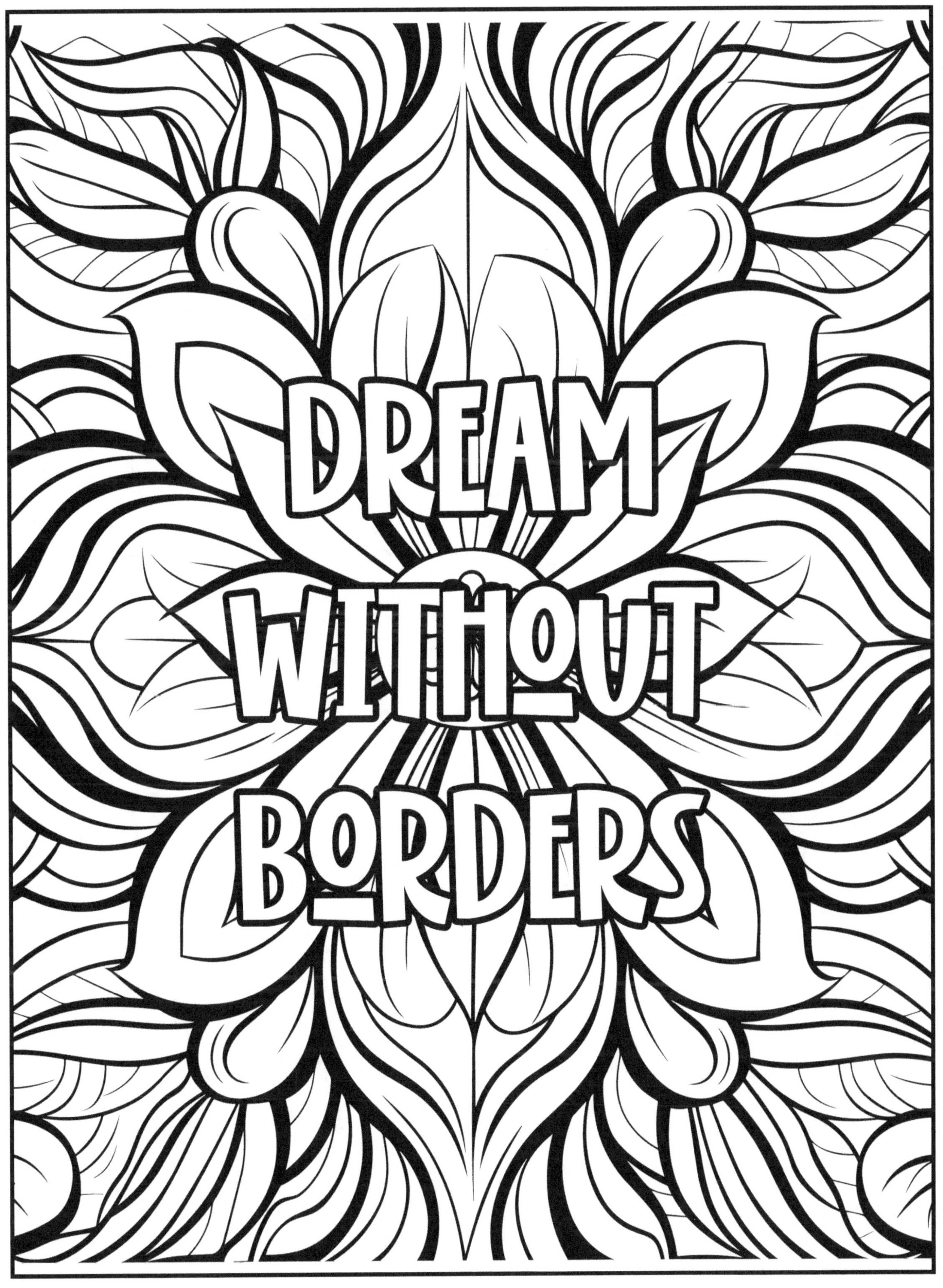

DREAM
WITHOUT
BORDERS

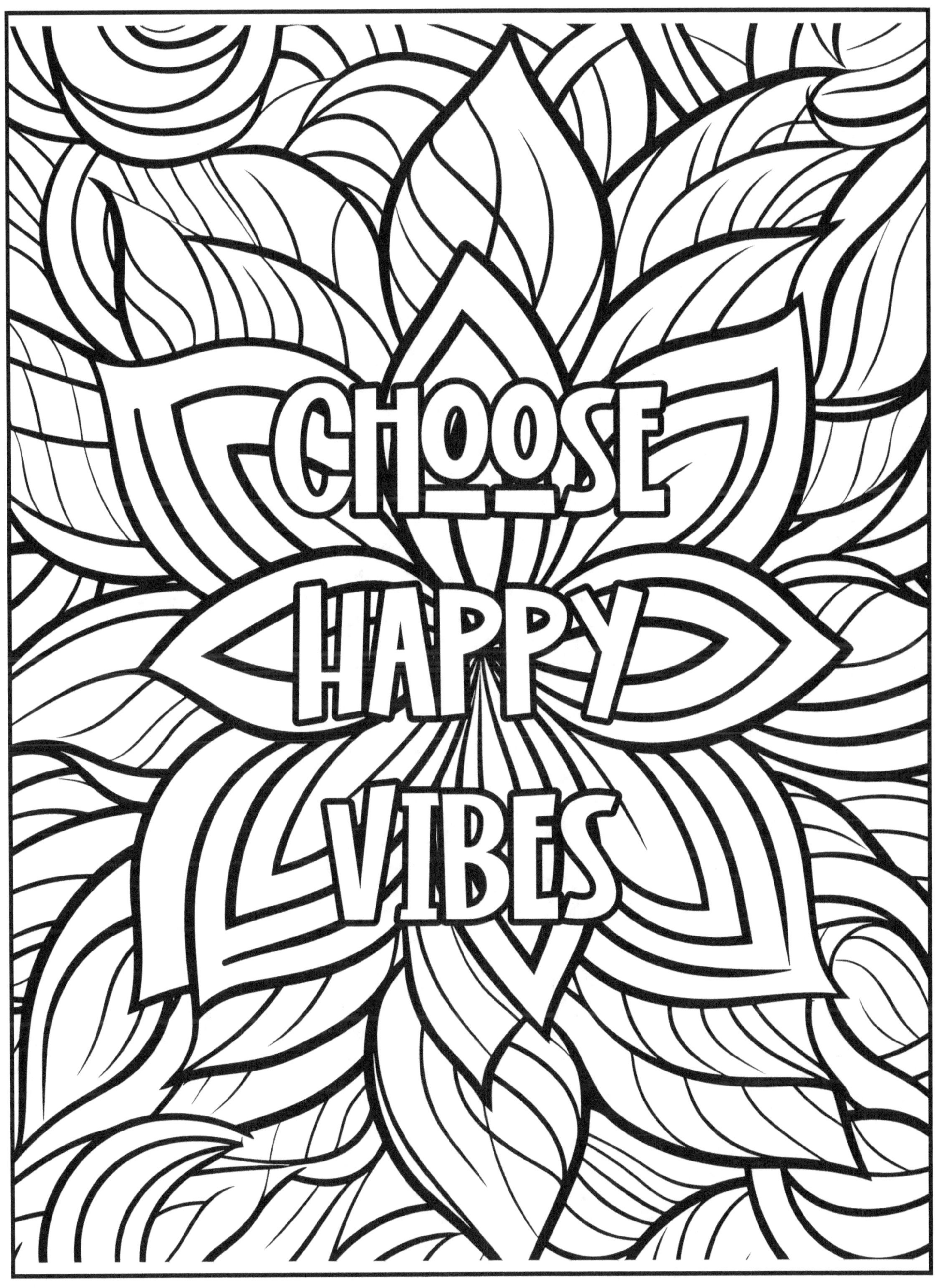
CHOOSE
HAPPY
VIBES

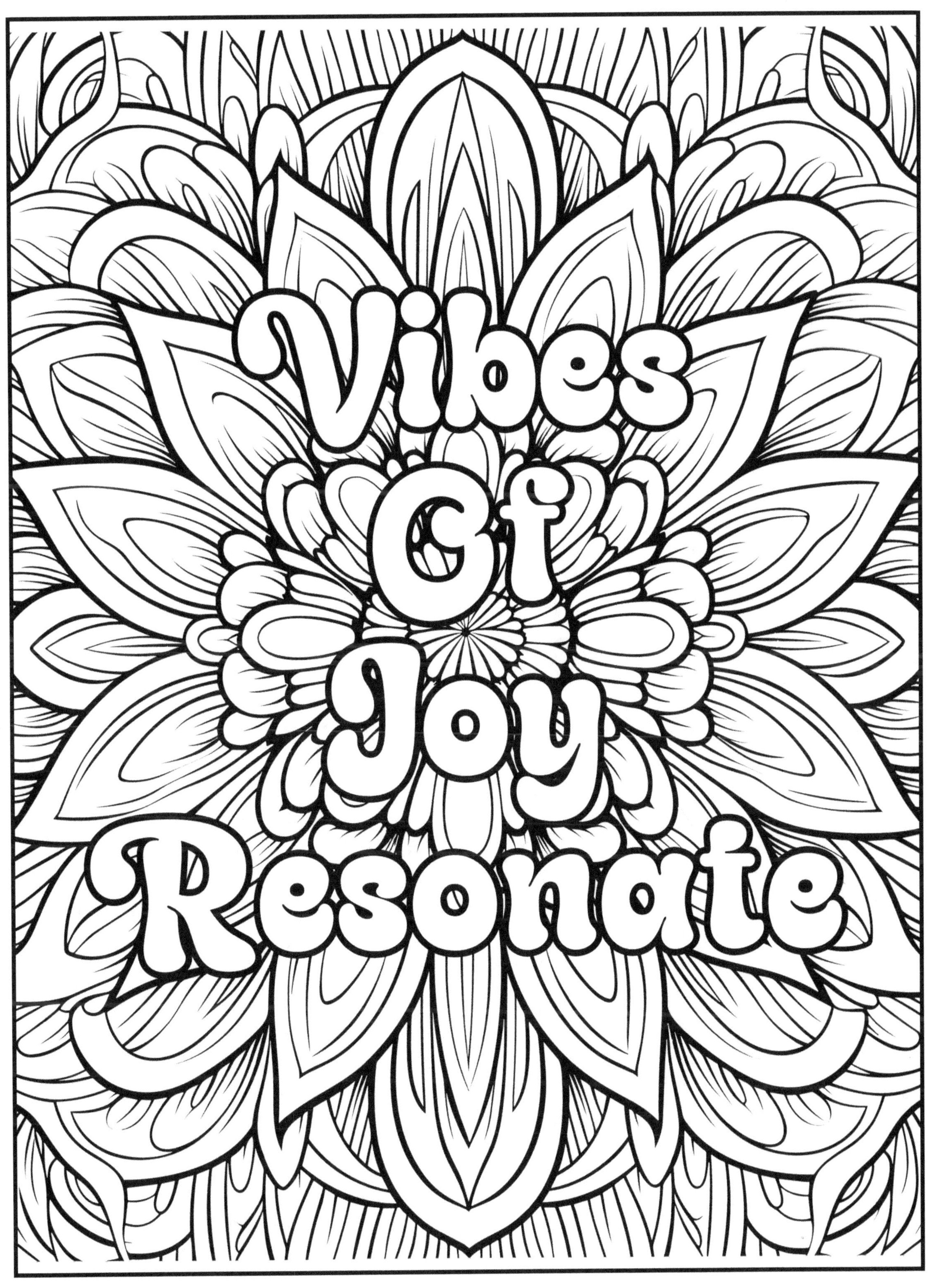

Vibes
Of
Joy
Resonate

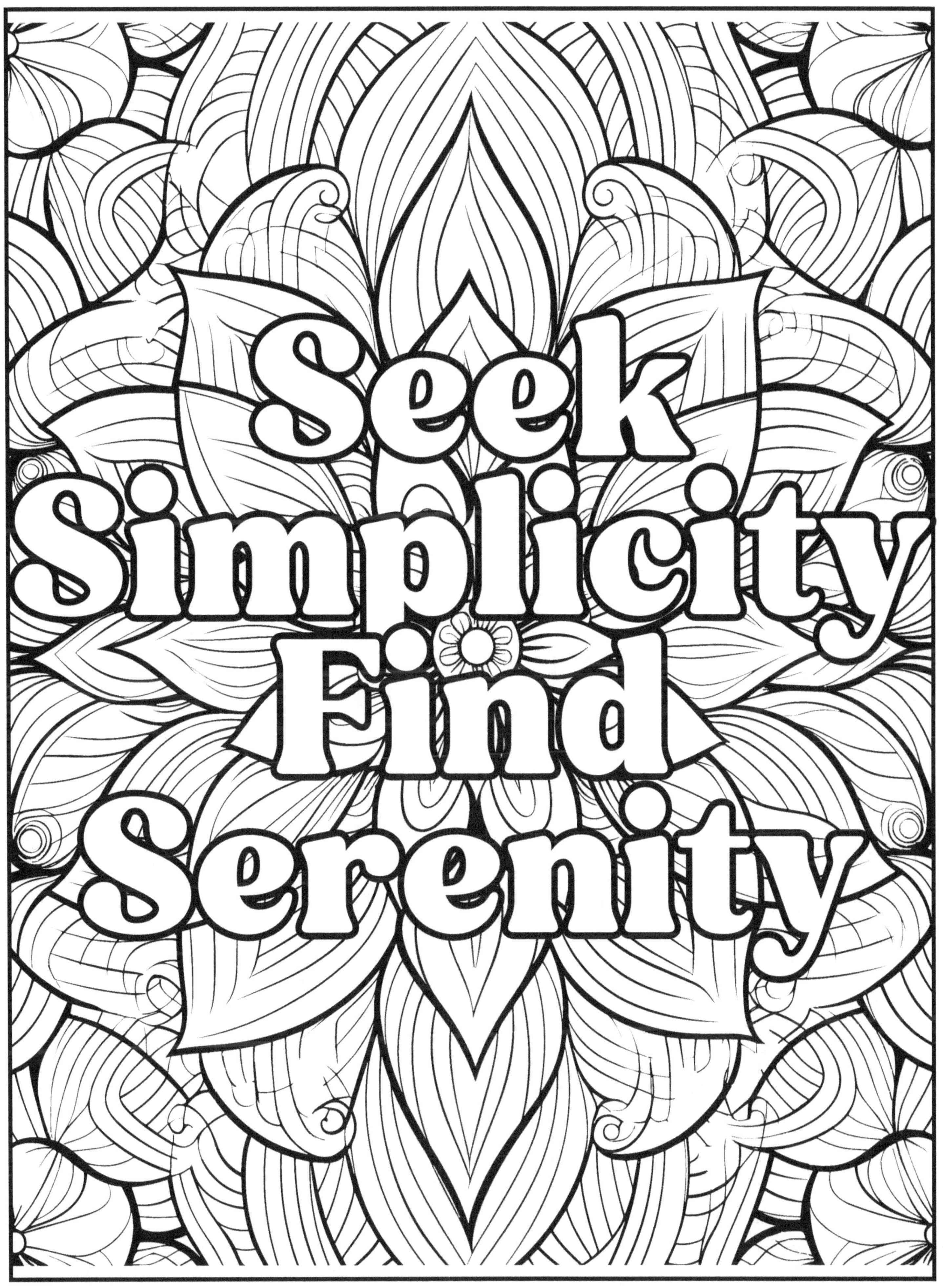
Seek
Simplicity
Find
Serenity

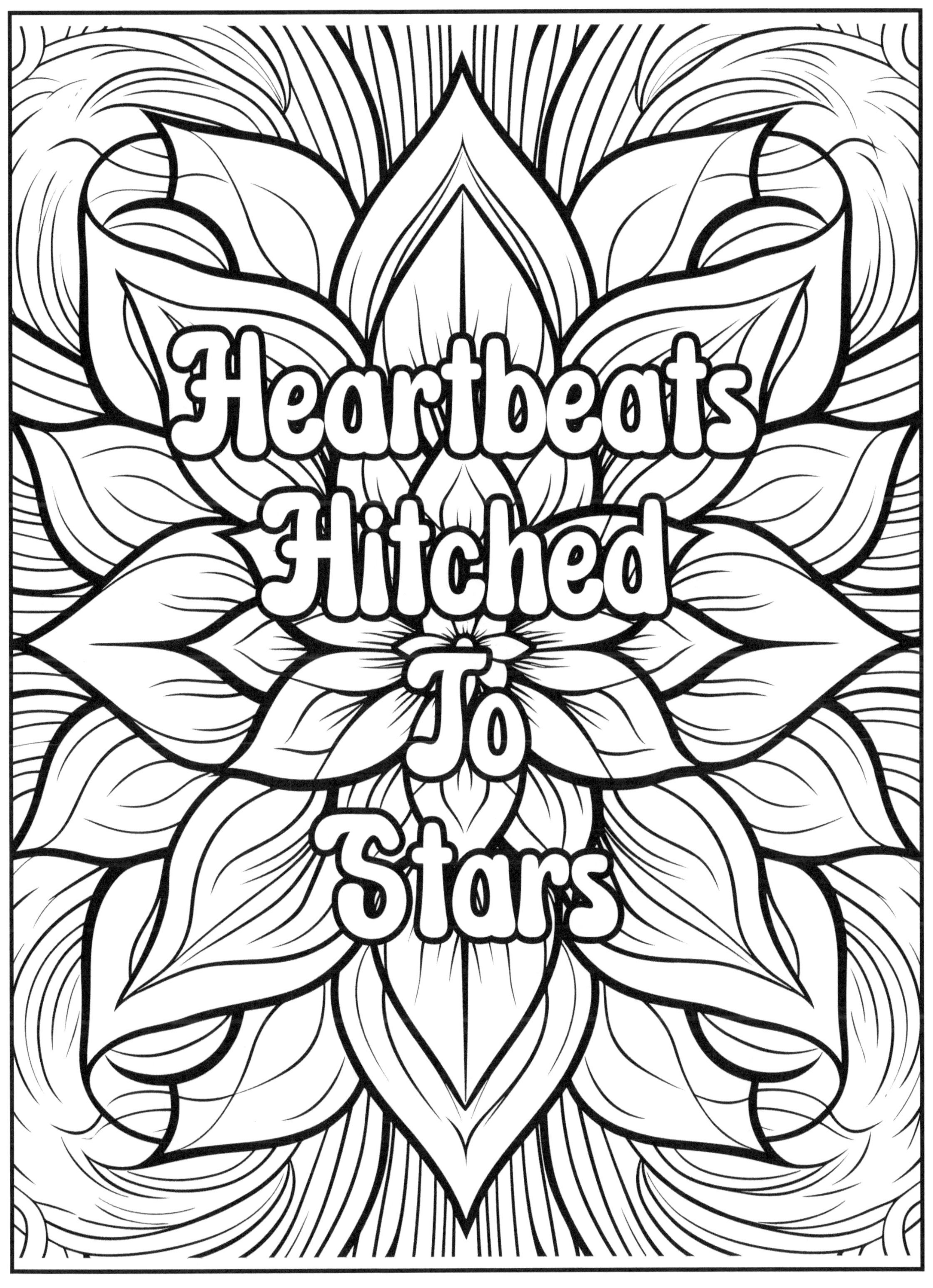
Heartbeats
Hitched
To
Stars

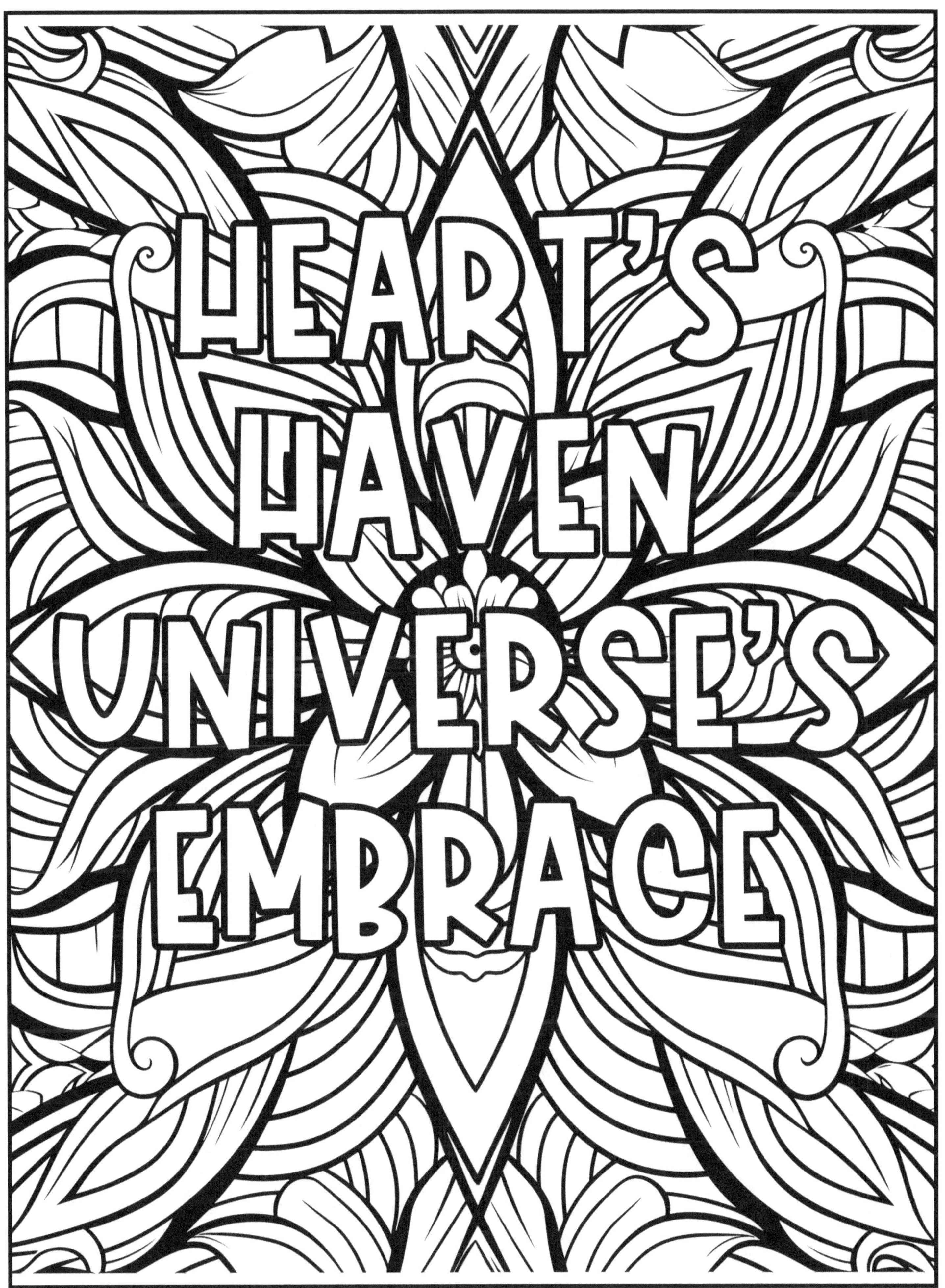

HEART'S
HAVEN
UNIVERSE'S
EMBRACE

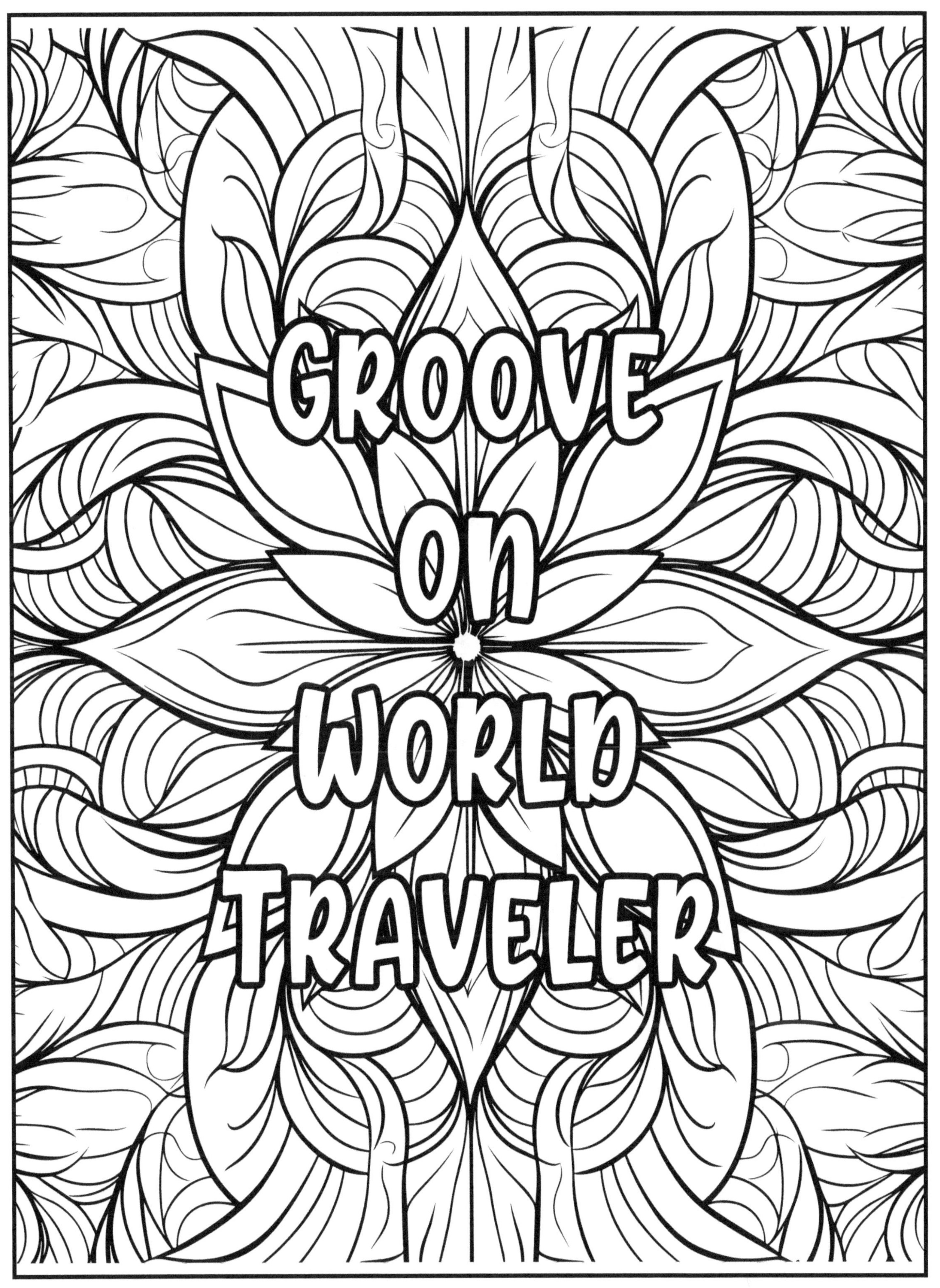

Groove
On
World
Traveler

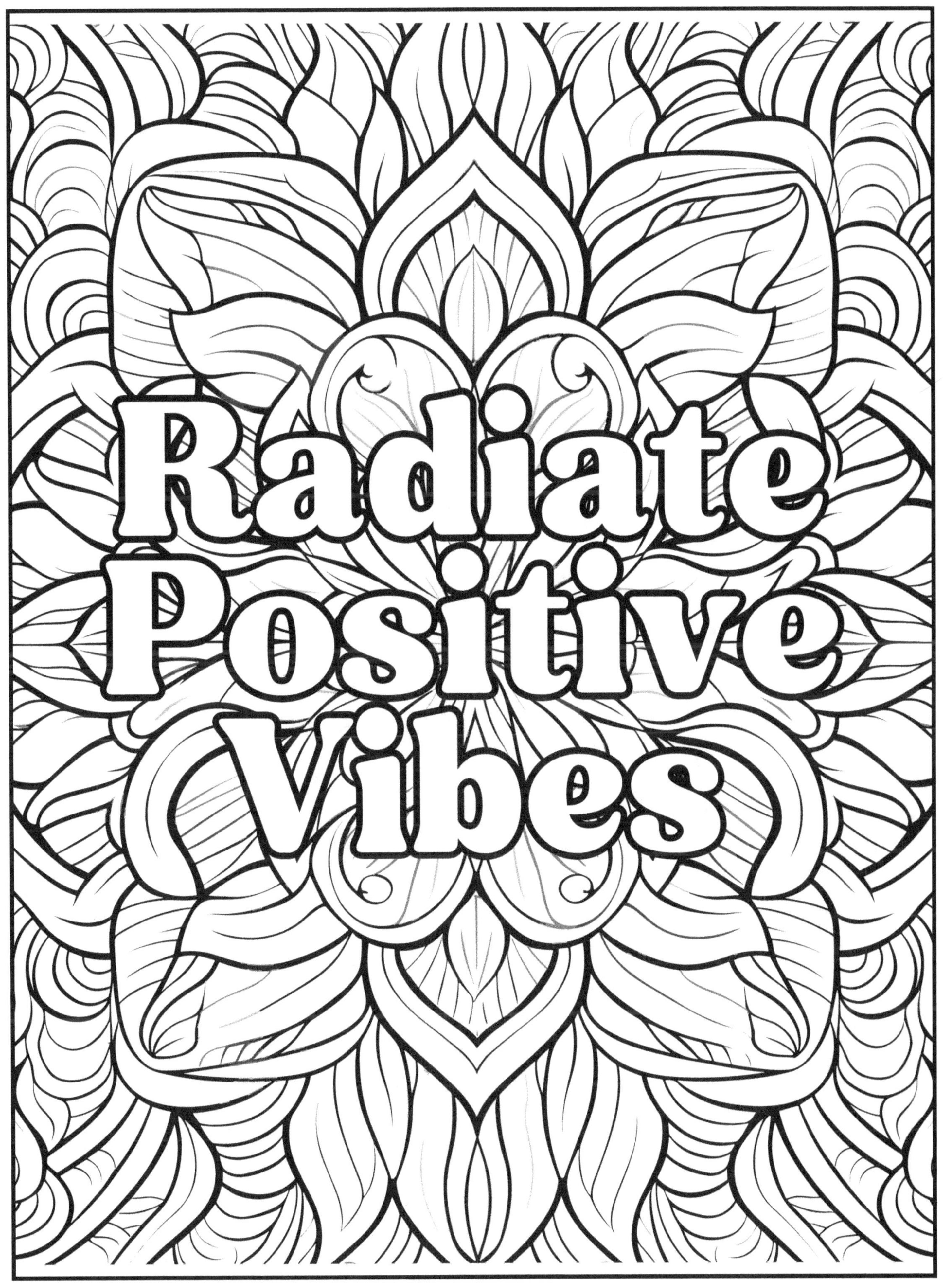
Radiate
Positive
Vibes

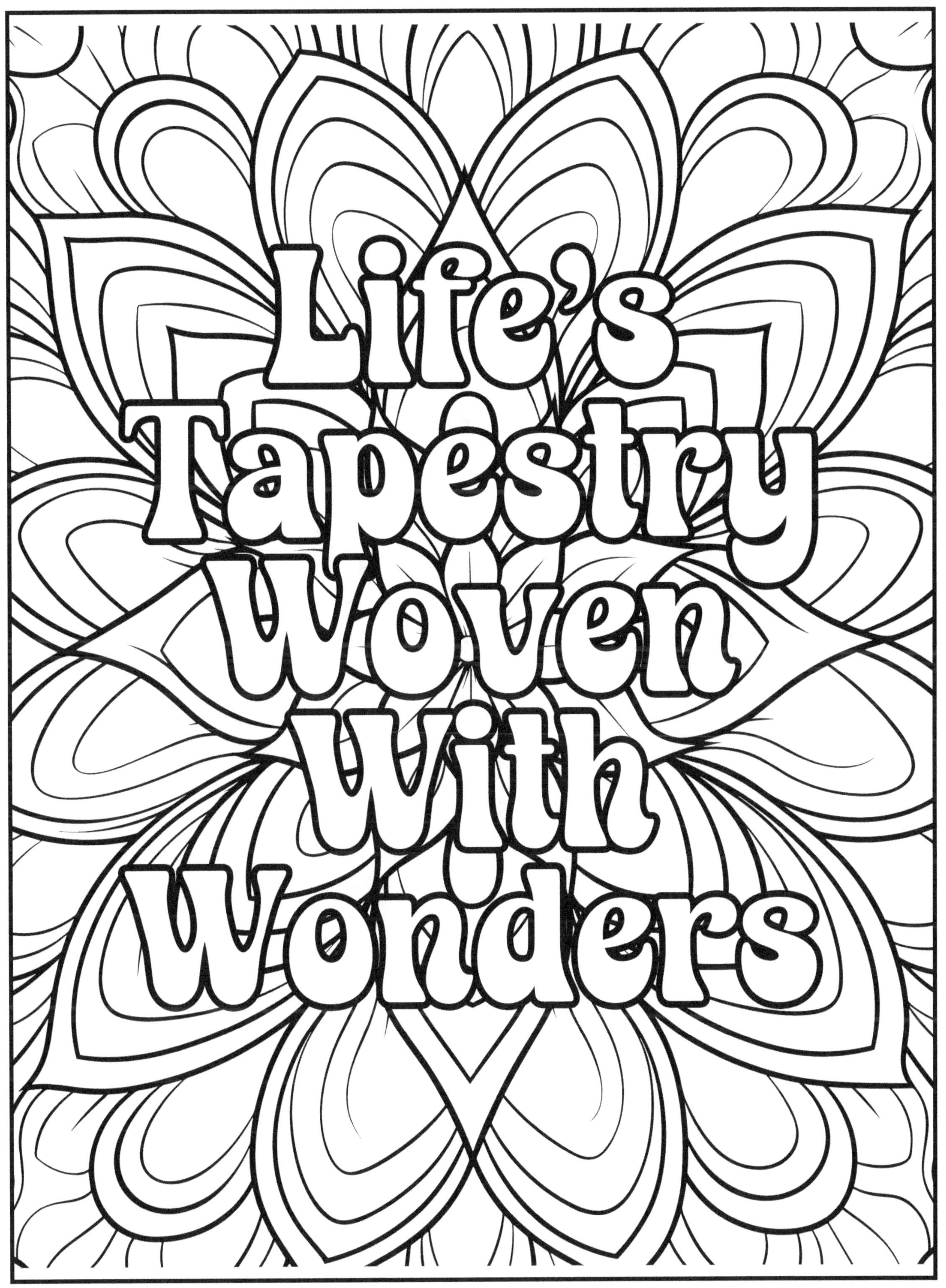

Life's
Tapestry
Woven
With
Wonders

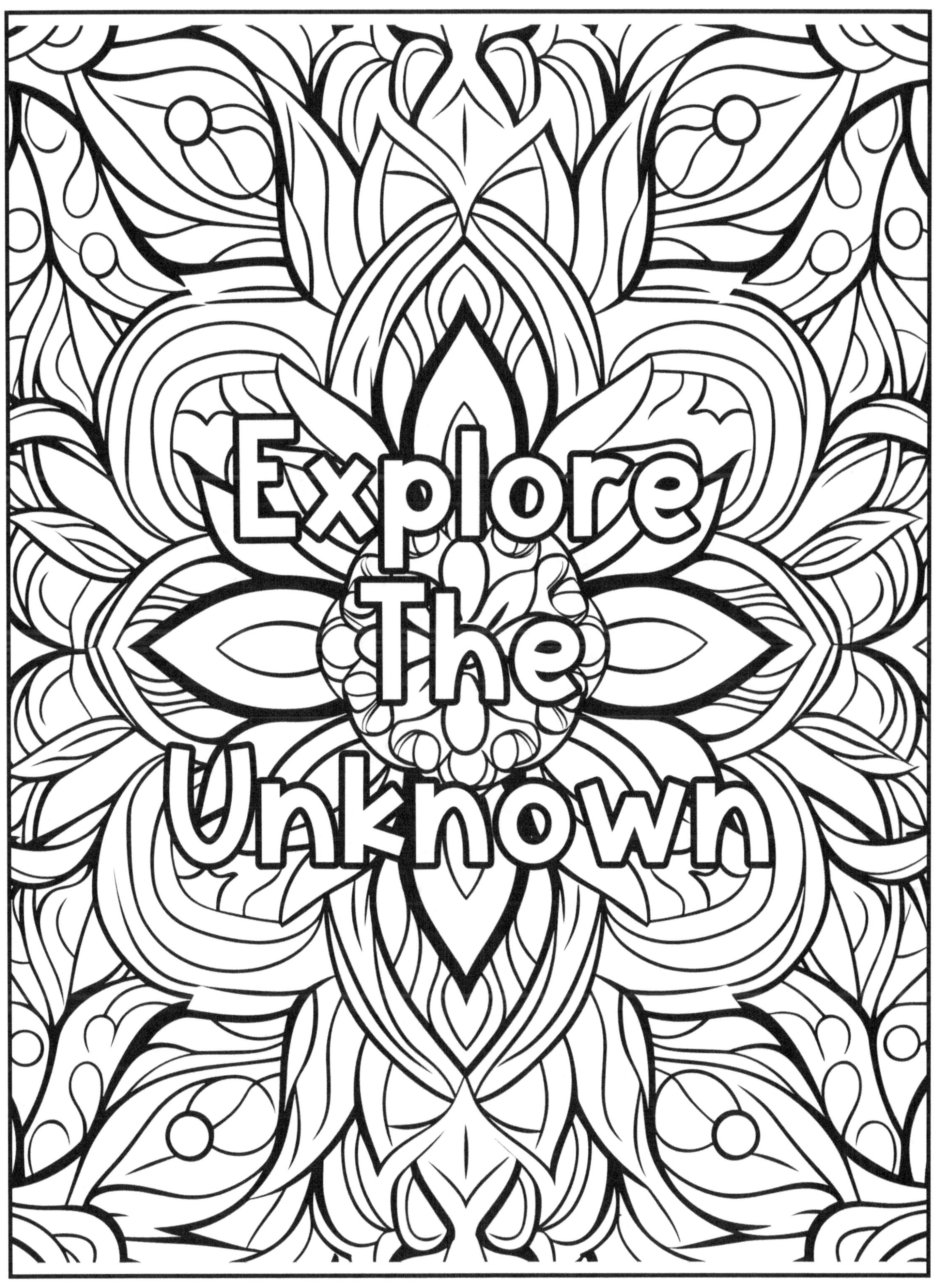
Explore
The
Unknown

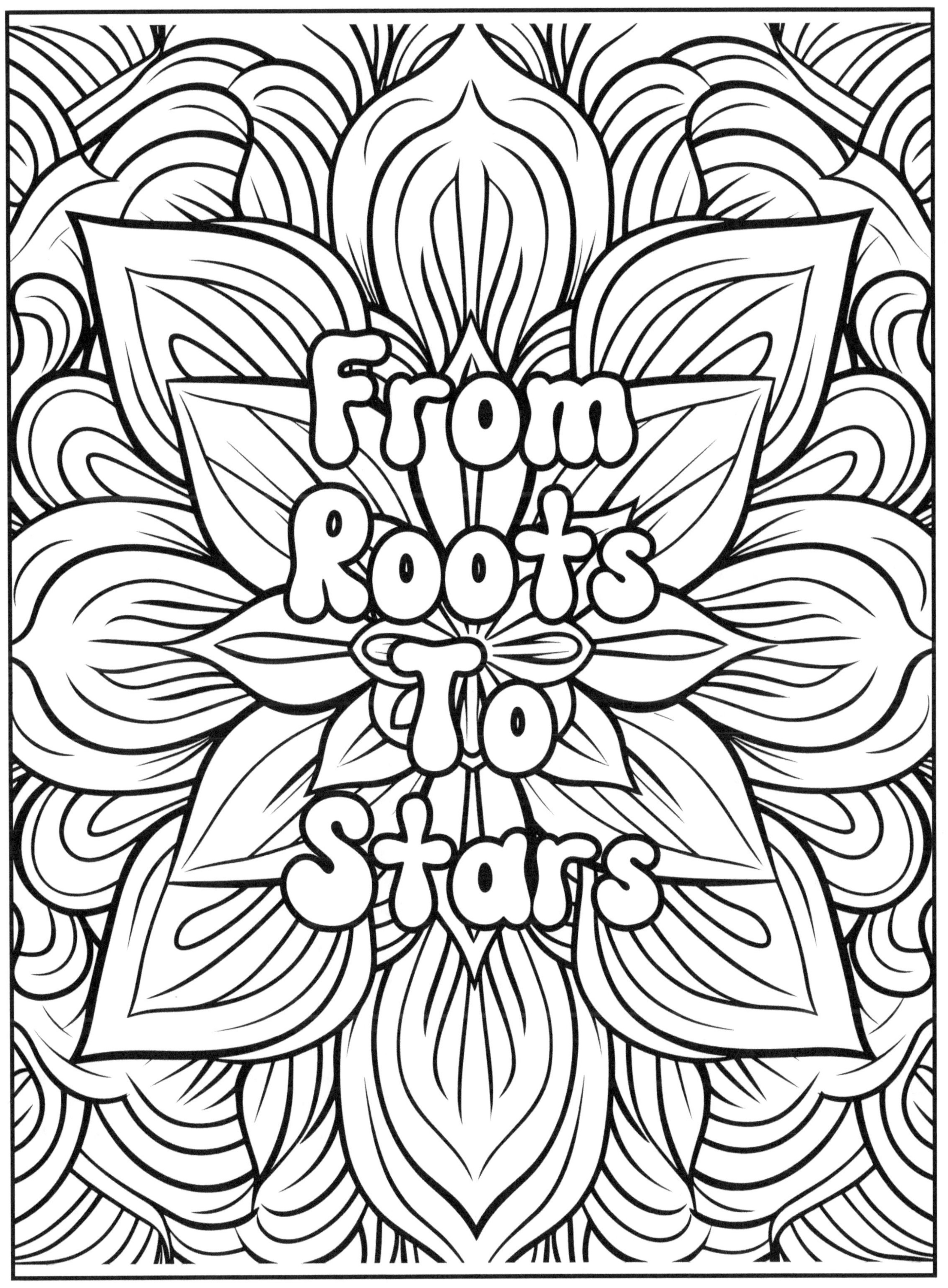
From
Roots
To
Stars

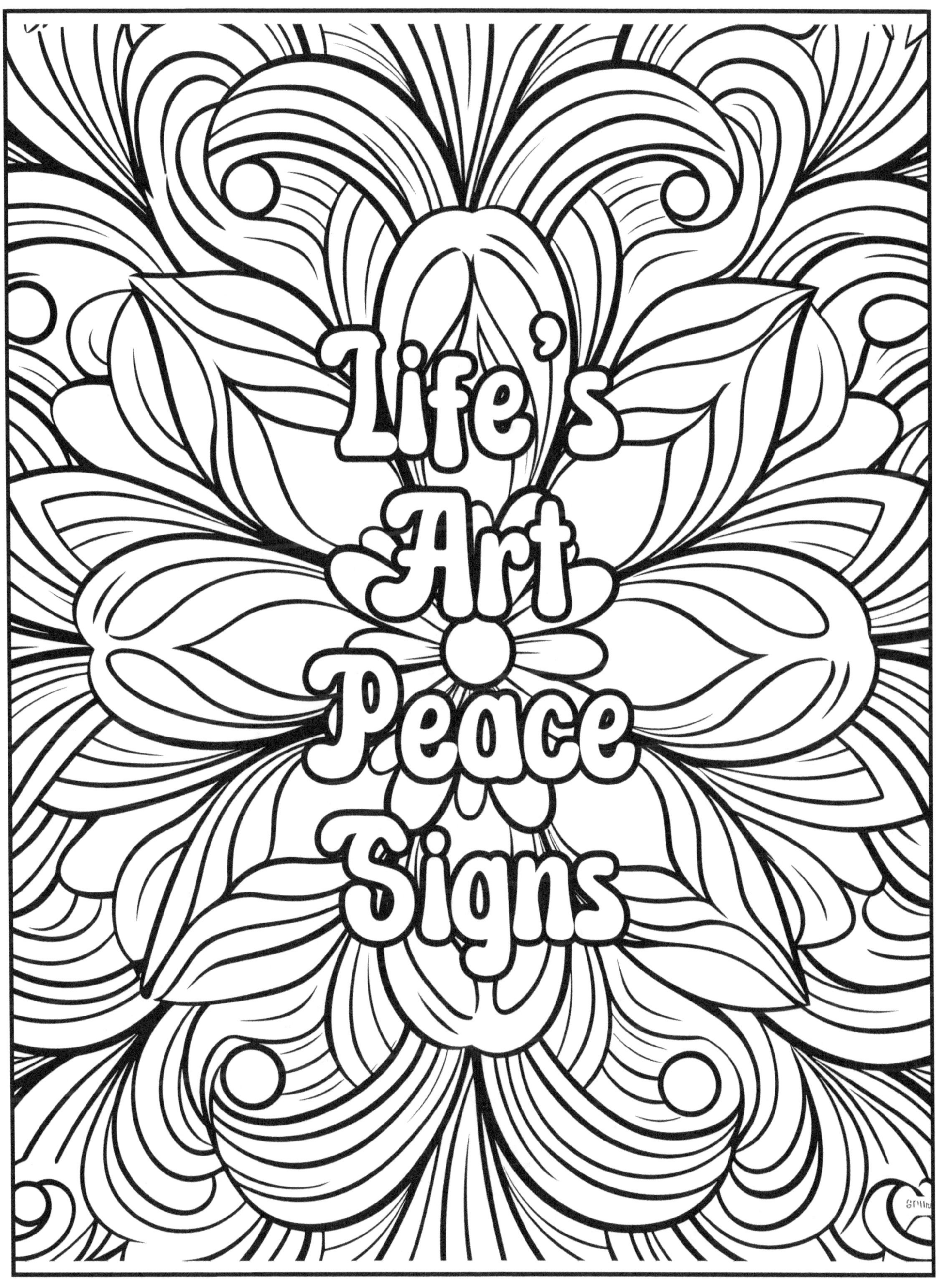

Life's
Art
Peace
Signs

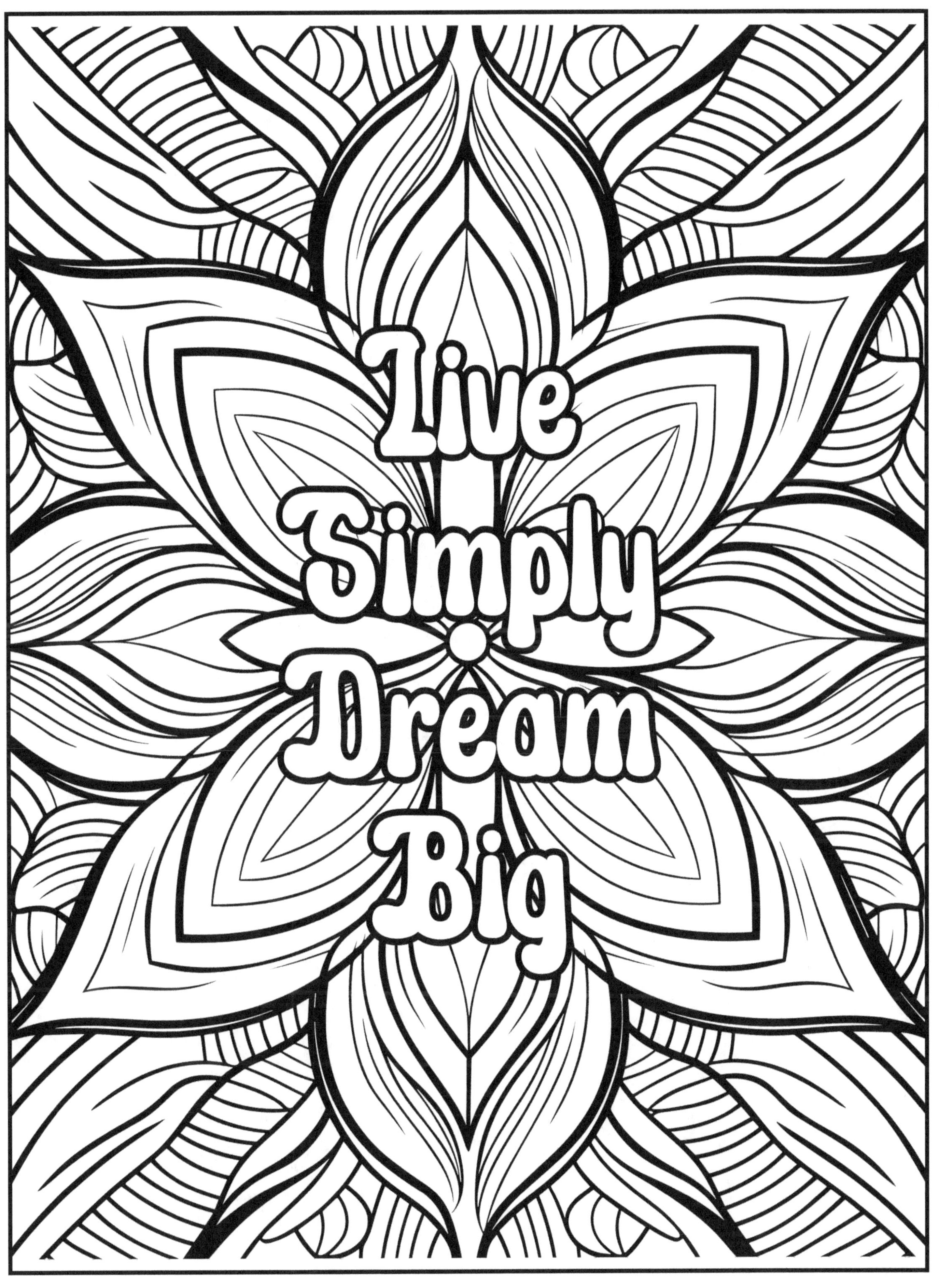

Live
Simply
Dream
Big

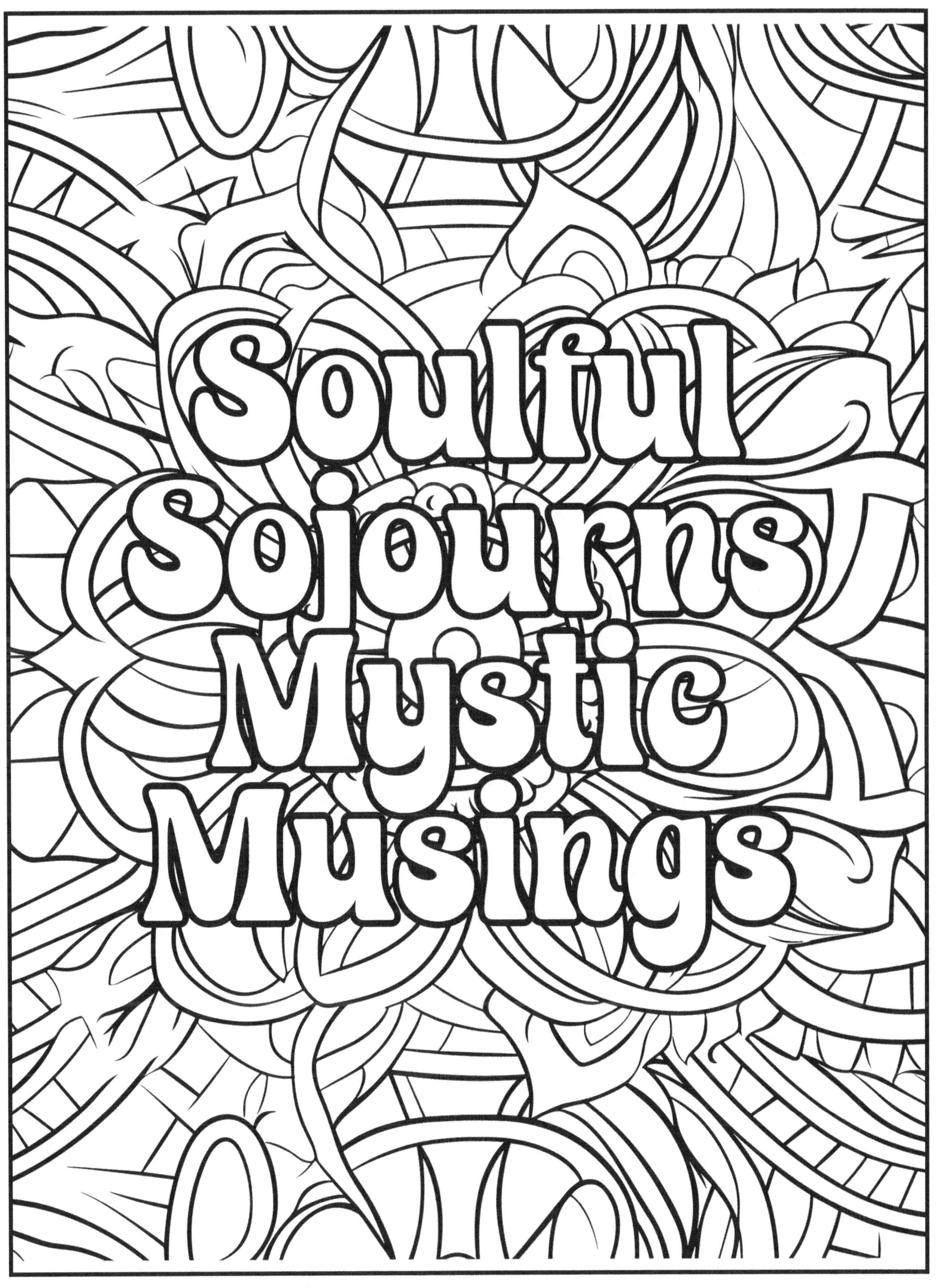

Soulful
Sojourns
Mystic
Musings

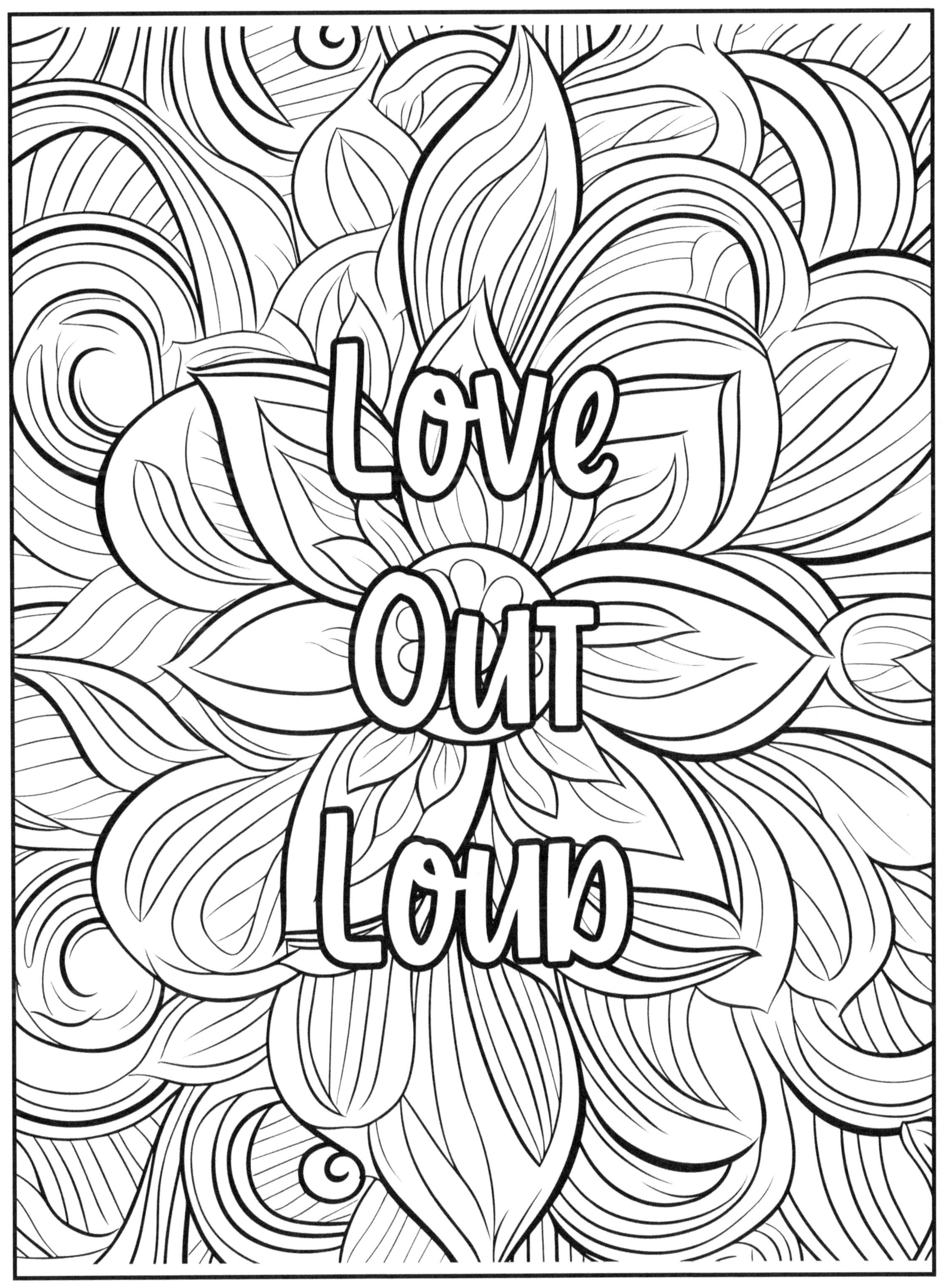

Love
Out
Loud

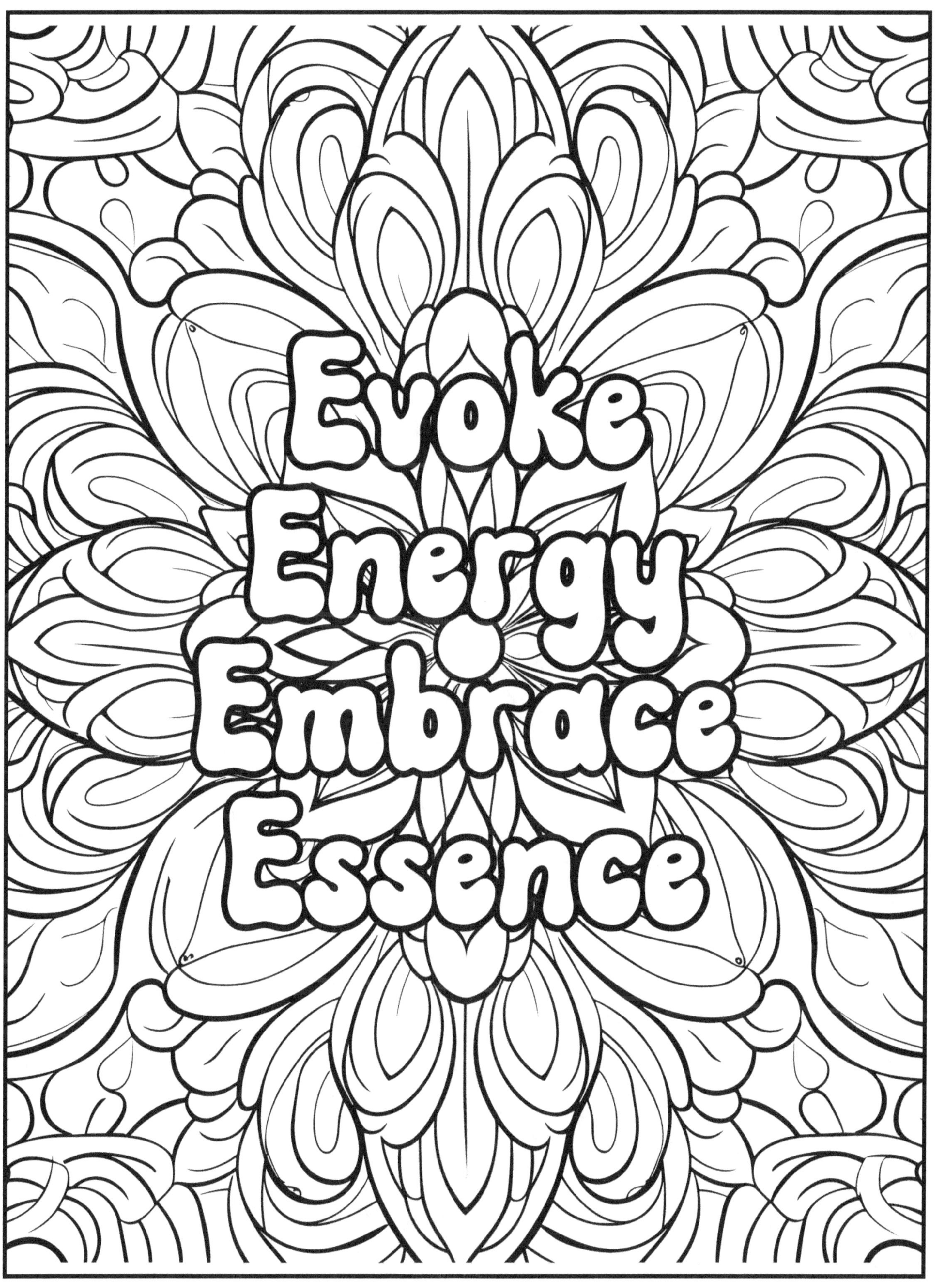

Evoke
Energy
Embrace
Essence

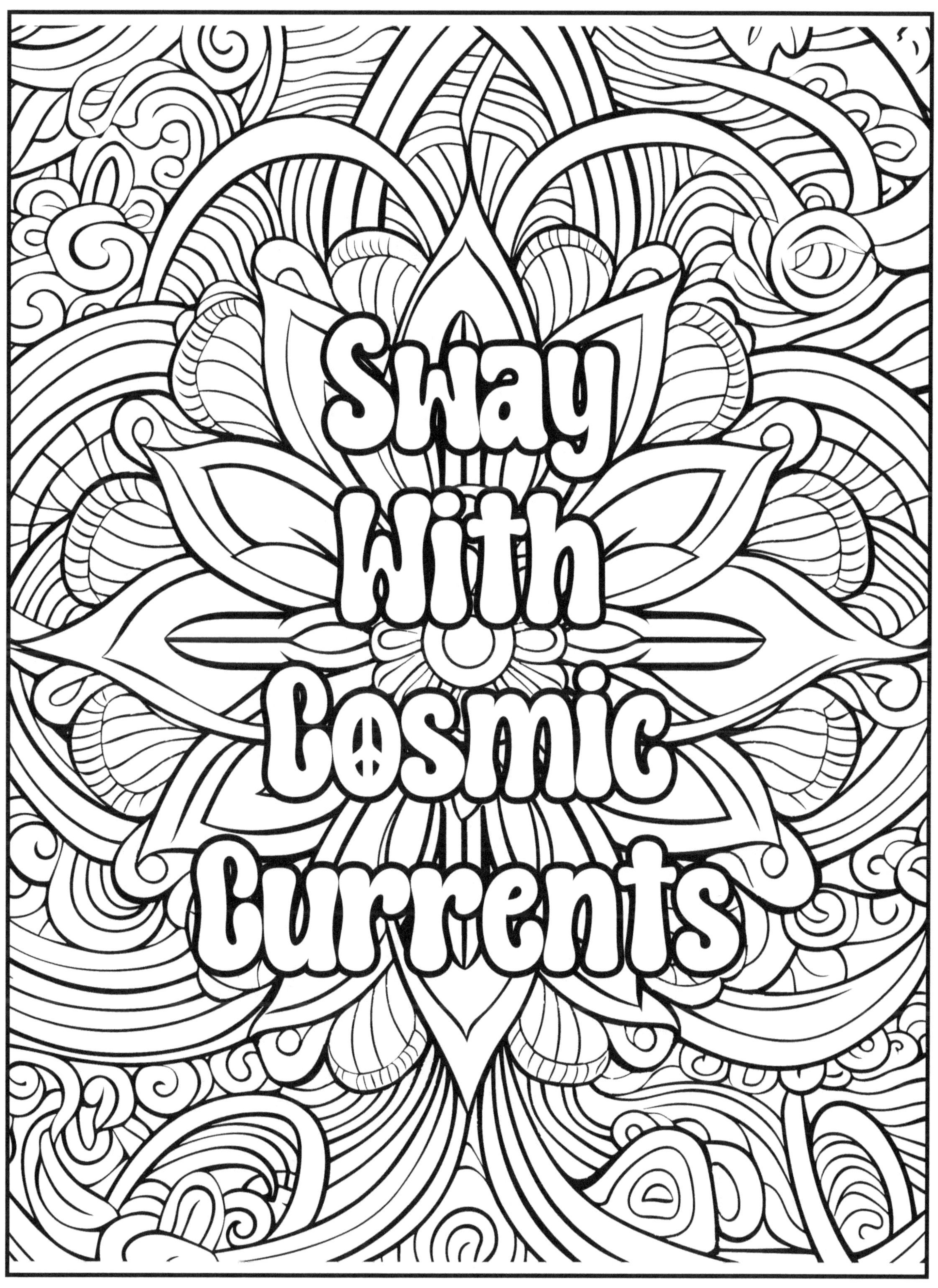

Sway
With
Cosmic
Currents

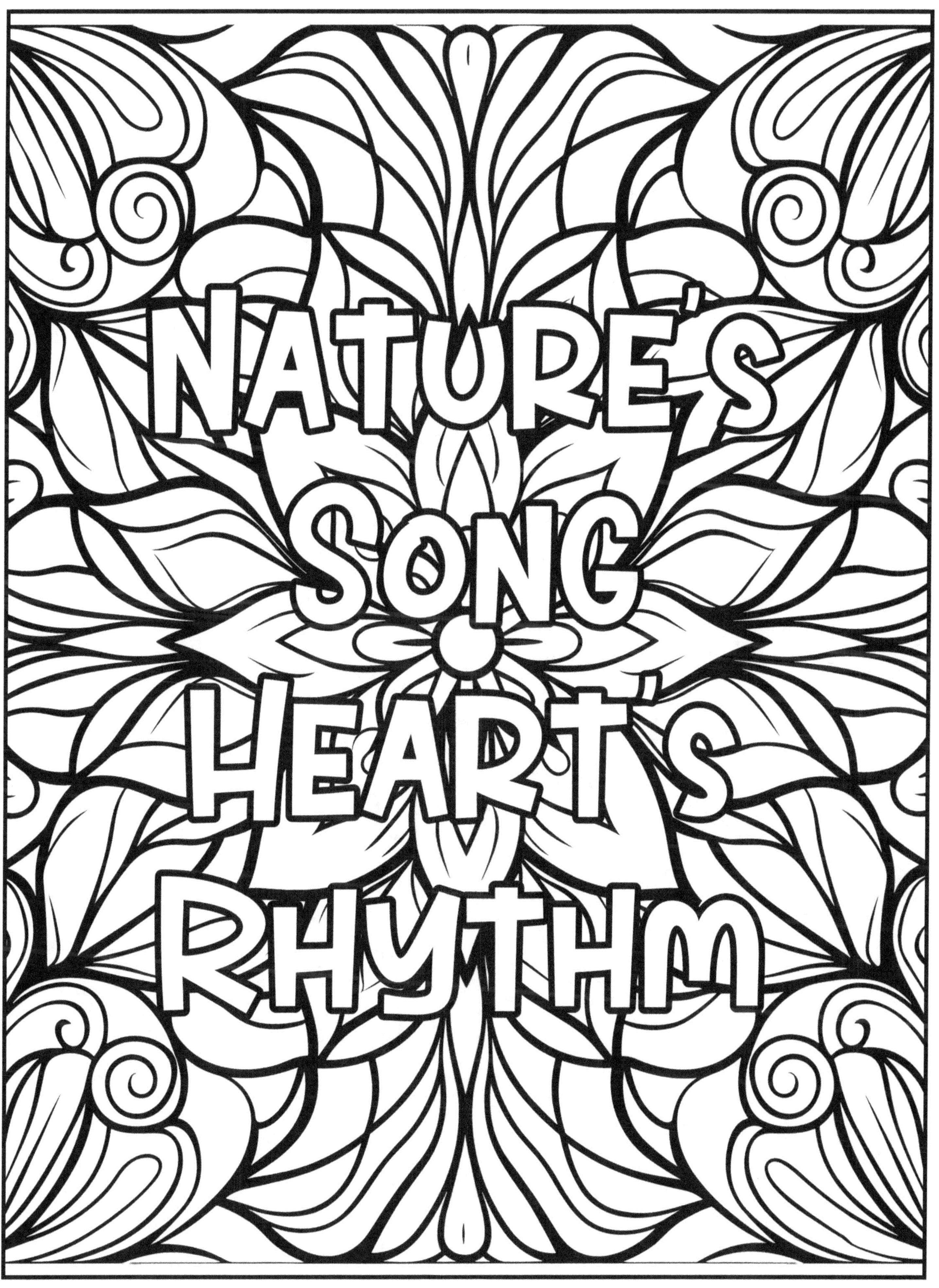
NATURE'S
SONG
HEART'S
RHYTHM

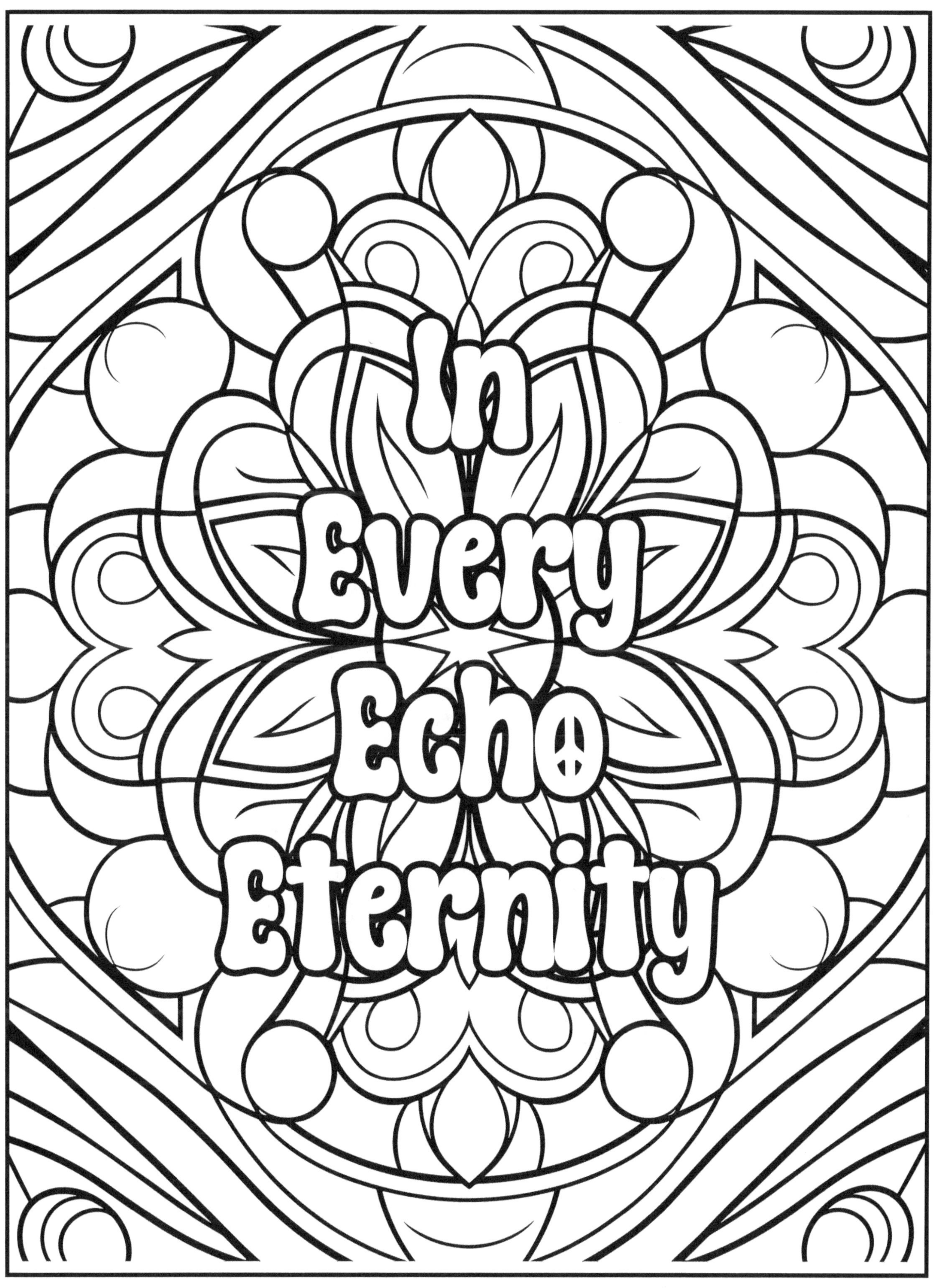
In
Every
Echo
Eternity

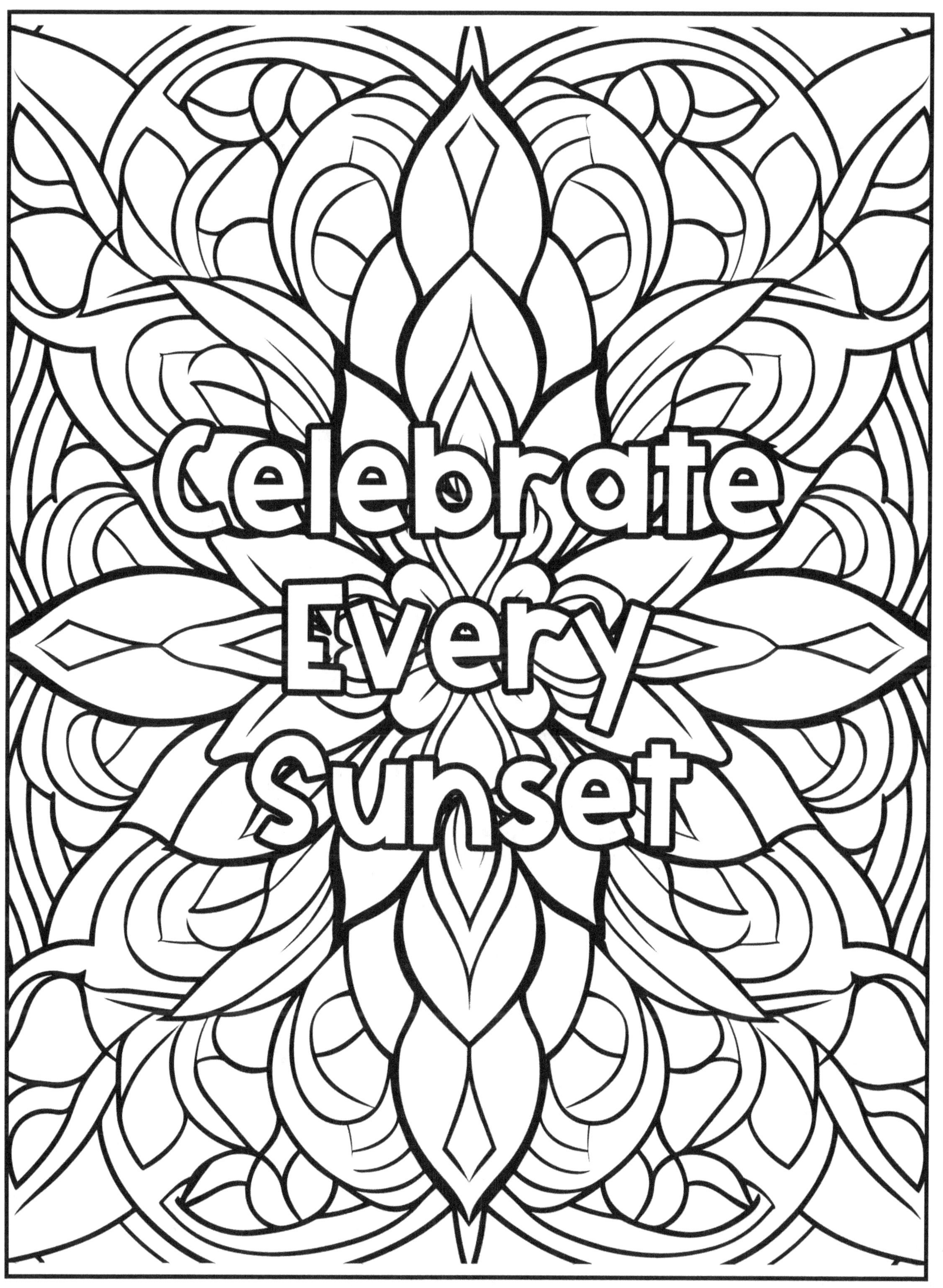

Celebrate
Every
Sunset